American Visionary Poetry

American Visionary Poetry

HYATT H. WAGGONER

LOUISIANA STATE UNIVERSITY PRESS
BATON ROUGE AND LONDON

Designer: Rod Parker
Typeface: Bembo
Typesetter: Graphic Composition, Inc.
Printer and Binder: Thomson-Shore

Library of Congress Cataloging in Publication Data

Waggoner, Hyatt Howe.
American visionary poetry.

Includes index.
1. American poetry—History and criticism.
2. Vision in literature. 3. Visual perception in literature. I. Title.
PS310.V57W33 1982   811'.009'1   82–8987
ISBN 0–8071–1051–5   AACR2

CONTENTS

Preface   vii

Acknowledgments   xi

Chapter I
Visionary Poetry: Learning to See   1

Chapter II
Walt Whitman: "I and the Old Round Earth"   25

Chapter III
Hart Crane: "Only in Darkness Is Thy Shadow
Clear"   67

Chapter IV
William Carlos Williams: Naturalizing the
Unearthly   89

Chapter V
Theodore Roethke: Learning to See in the Dark   113

Chapter VI
A. R. Ammons: Ezra "Perishing for Deity"   143

Chapter VII
David Wagoner: "Traveling Light"   179

Chapter VIII
Prospects   199

Appendix:
Seeing and Believing—
Dickinson, Frost, Eliot, Stevens   209

Index   219

PREFACE

The earliest of the essays that make up this little book was prompted by my dissatisfaction with what seemed to me the loose, almost meaningless, use of the word *visionary* by contemporary critics to describe poets whose work appeared to have little or nothing in common. But it rather quickly became apparent that my plea for clarity in the use of the word opened up at least as many questions as it closed, so I was led to reexamine the work of some poets who might clarify the abstract definitions I had proposed. What began as a talk at a Brown University colloquium became the introductory chapter, with the essays that follow written in the order in which they appear.

The explicit argument of this book—that we should think of "visionary poetry" as a genre with certain definable characteristics that can be tested and found present or wanting—may well seem acceptable enough even if the conclusions arrived at seem wrongheaded, or incomplete, or both. About the incompleteness of this study there is no question. The essays were never intended as an exhaustive or definitive treatment of visionary poetry—as I see it, that would be a job for a lifetime. So far as these essays on certain American poets carry conviction, they open a subject for inquiry; they do not close it.

More specifically, they leave wide open a number of very important questions. For instance, is visionary poetry as I propose that we define it primarily a cultural symptom destined to disappear as culture changes? It presumably would not exist in a tribal society, but what about its future in the "developed" nations? Can visionary poetry accommodate the machine, as Hart Crane tried to, and flourish in a society dominated by computerized technology, or must the poets who write the visionary poems of the future turn to Nature for their inspiration, as Theodore Roethke, A. R. Ammons, David Wagoner, and others have done?

Religious and philosophical questions are similarly raised but not answered. Is visionary poetry a by-product of liberal Protestantism, as there seems to be some reason to think? But if so, how do we account for the poetry of Gerard Manley Hopkins? It would seem that adherence to a rigidly doctrinal church that claims to provide all the answers to questions of the meaning of life would at least discourage if not rule out the genre. Or again, what is the relationship, if any, between visionary poetry and mysticism, as defined by the various students of the subject?

But not every such question that might be asked is left open this way. Calvinism, with its sharp dualisms between body and spirit and between this world and the next, its doctrine of "total depravity," and its insistence that revelation is available only in Scriptural Revelation, seems to me to make visionary poems unthinkable. Similarly, doctrinaire "Naturalism" of the type described and rejected by Alfred North Whitehead a long generation ago—with its scientific positivism, its mechanistic materialism, and its vision of a "dead nature" in which life is a mysterious sport—rigidly adhered to, would seem to rule out the possibility of a poet's writing a visionary poem as I have defined and illustrated the genre. So too would total skepticism of the sort that denies the possibility of our knowing or saying anything at all about the reality outside the mind. Visionary poetry can live with the uncertainty principle but not with total skepticism—or with the belief of many of the newest critics that poetry is not "about" anything, but is only a language game that opens no window on reality. I may of course be wrong about such matters, but at least the essays that follow do not leave these questions open.

★   ★   ★

I am indebted to my former colleague in the Psychology Department at Brown, Loren Riggs, who guided me to the best recent books from the vision laboratories; to Austin Warren, who read the manuscript as it was produced, found it stimulating, and kept asking me the most difficult questions to answer; and to Howard Munford, who also read the text and encouraged me to believe I was onto something worth pursuing.

ACKNOWLEDGMENTS

Chapter I herein was originally published, in somewhat different form, as "Visionary Poetry: Learning to See," in *Sewanee Review*, 79 (Spring, 1981). Copyright © 1981 by Hyatt H. Waggoner. It is reprinted here with the gracious permission of the *Sewanee Review*.

Selections from William Carlos Williams, *Collected Earlier Poems* (copyright 1938 by New Directions Publishing Corporation), from *Collected Later Poems* (copyright 1948 by William Carlos Williams), from *Pictures from Brueghel and Other Poems* (copyright © 1955 by William Carlos Williams), and from *Paterson* (copyright 1949 by William Carlos Williams) are all reprinted by permission of New Directions Publishing Corporation.

Poetic excerpts from *The Collected Poems of Theodore Roethke*, copyright © 1937, 1954, 1957, 1958, 1959, 1960, 1961, 1962, 1963, 1964, 1965, 1966 by Beatrice Roethke as Administratrix of the Estate of Theodore Roethke; copyright © 1932, 1934, 1935, 1936, 1937, 1938, 1939, 1940, 1941, 1942, 1946, 1947, 1948, 1949, 1950, 1951, 1952, 1953, 1954, 1955, 1956, 1957, 1958, 1961 by Theodore Roethke. Reprinted by permission of Doubleday & Company, Inc., and of Faber and Faber, Ltd. "Night Crow" copyright 1944 by Saturday Review Association, Inc. "Big Wind" copyright 1947 by The United Chapters of Phi Beta Kappa.

Selections from David Wagoner, *Landfall: Poems* (copyright © 1980, 1981 by David Wagoner) reprinted by permission of Little, Brown and Company in association with the Atlantic Monthly Press. "Landfall" by David Wagoner reprinted from *Prairie Schooner* by permission of University of Nebraska Press. Copyright © 1980 by University of Nebraska Press. Selections from David Wagoner, *Collected Poems 1956–1976* (copyright © 1976 by Indiana University Press) reprinted by permission of Indiana University Press.

Lines from Allen Ginsberg, "Footnote to Howl" from *Howl & Other Poems* (copyright © 1956, 1959 by Allen Ginsberg) reprinted by permission of City Lights Books.

Selections from *Complete Poems and Selected Letters and Prose of Hart Crane*, edited by Brom Weber, copyright 1933, copyright © 1958, 1966 by Liveright Publishing Corporation, reprinted by permission of the Liveright Publishing Corporation and W. W. Norton Company, Inc.

Acknowledgment is made to W. W. Norton Company, Inc., New York, for permission to quote from:

Diversifications, Poems, by A. R. Ammons, copyright © 1975 by A. R. Ammons;

A Coast of Trees, Poems, by A. R. Ammons, copyright © 1981 by A. R. Ammons;

Sphere: The Form of a Motion, by A. R. Ammons, copyright © 1974 by A. R. Ammons;

Collected Poems, 1951–1971, by A. R. Ammons, copyright © 1972 by A. R. Ammons;

Tape for the Turn of the Year, by A. R. Ammons, copyright © 1965 by Cornell University.

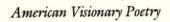

American Visionary Poetry

CHAPTER I

Visionary Poetry: Learning to See

"And God said, Let there be light: and there was light. And God saw the light, that it was good."
        —*Genesis 1:2–3*

"After these things the word of the Lord came unto Abram in a vision."
        —*Genesis 15:1*

"Where there is no vision, the people perish."
        —*Proverbs 29:18*

"And, like the baseless fabric of this vision. . . . shall dissolve."
        —*The Tempest*, IV, 1

"Seeing is believing," we say, and "out of sight, out of mind," while knowing that there are optical illusions and distrusting those "visionaries" who confuse the products of wish and imagination with reality. Is the visionary then a mere dreamer or a true seer? Are his visions apparitions or revelations, delusions or epiphanies?

Although past usage of *visionary* leaves such questions open, today's usage seems increasingly to favor the positive sense of the word, the "visionary" as one who sees better or farther, deeper or more truly, than we. If the politicians and the scientists, or both working together, cannot save us, perhaps those less practical friends and aiders of those who would live in the spirit, the poets, can provide us with a vision we can trust and live with.

So Blake, Wordsworth, Yeats, Emerson, Whitman, Stevens, and a host of lesser figures are all praised as "visionaries," without its becoming at all clear what they have in common. A good many of the best-known contemporary poets produce verse that is quasi-religious in tone and reminiscent of myth in vocabulary, and we like to honor their work too by calling it "visionary," though it may express only nostalgia or despair and have little or no reference to any reality outside the poet's mind.

Indiscriminate use of a word can destroy its usefulness. *Visionary* is potentially too useful a word to be dropped from our vocabulary, but can we agree on a meaning for it that can apply to poetry? Poet X was a true visionary, I say, but Poet Y a deluded dreamer and Poet Z a disappointed idealist who felt, mistakenly, that honesty required that he make do with a shrunken vision. We will agree, no doubt—when we can share a common conception of "reality." Unfortunately, we may not be around to welcome that distant day. Is there any way of agreeing, at least tentatively and provisionally, on what the marks of visionary poetry are, while continuing to disagree on the nature of ultimate reality and reserving the right to make our own choices of which "visionary" poets are the ones whose vision we can share, and therefore call "true vision"?

What I propose is that we reattach *visionary*, that figurative, richly ambiguous word, to its root in *vision*—that is, at the most literal level, to the act of seeing, as in the expression "he has 20/20 vision." Some of us have clear vision, some blurred, and not only for organic or somatic reasons having to do with the structure of the eye or brain. It seems to me possible to do this now, as it would not have been a half century ago, in terms that are consistent with what is known about how we literally do "see"—*i.e.*, with the results of experimentation in the vision laboratories. And if possible, this definition should have certain advantages, at least for those who find themselves dissatisfied with interpretations that make the visionary equivalent to the "imagined" or "dreamed"—constructed or projected, but not discovered— yet find themselves unable to accept the romantic "Metaphysical Idealism" that once served Emerson and others as foundation for a noetic conception of the poet's visionary role. To do this would not belittle the imagination, for it turns out that imagination is required really to see even the "literal," interpreting what is present to the senses in terms of what is present in the mind only.

★   ★   ★

Normally, when someone says, "Look! Do you see what I see?" we look, and either see the thing or don't. If we don't, it may be because our own vision is defective—we are nearsighted, perhaps—or because we don't know what to look for, having never seen anything resembling what our friend thinks he sees; or it may be that there is really nothing there and our friend is just "seeing things."

The question of course is whether anything analogous to this situation arises when we read visionary poetry. Must we be content with the view that the visionary poet is projecting his personal neurotic needs, or the residue of the Collective Unconscious, onto a neutral, or at least unknowable, reality? Or else that he is imagining, and thus creating in the poem—but only in the poem—order and meaning, when in fact, "in reality," there is only disorder and no meaning? In short, does visionary poetry—when we judge that it speaks to our condition—tell us anything about "reality," say to us "Look—and you'll see," like our friend; or is it to be thought of as not "about" anything? More abstractly put, does, or can, poetry convey knowledge, or does it give us merely a pleasurable, but purely "aesthetic"—that is, without truth-value—experience? In terms of the mind-matter, subjective-objective dualisms that have largely structured Western thought since Descartes, must we say that visionary poetry has only subjective value?

Of course, the way I have put these questions implies what I think the answers should be. I think poetry, including the kind of poetry we want to call "visionary," can have—and does have *for* us when it speaks *to* us—the kind of cognitive value our friend's "Look!" has: either there is something there to be seen or there isn't. If we can't see what he says *he* sees, we have to decide whether our vision is defective or whether he is "just imagining" something not there. The truth-value of each "Look!" statement must be decided separately, though of course we come to expect some speakers—and some poets—to lie, or to try to trick us, or to suffer from hallucinations.

I should like to put aside, for now, the larger philosophic problems, both epistemological and ontological, raised by such questions and such answers in order to try to arrive at an acceptable working definition of *visionary* as applied to poetry by talking about poetry. If *visionary* is to be kept related to what can be perceived, and yet to retain the positive implications of better, deeper, truer, more imaginative perception, with the consequent discovery of patterns of meaning and value not easily perceived by most of us most of the time, many questions arise. Are the images that come in dreams, or in a dreamlike state, ruled out by the requirement that what is imaged be "visually perceptible"? Is "Kubla Khan" a "visionary" poem? (I'd be glad to "pass" on this one, but I'll say no.) Is what is seen in mystic vision to be similarly excluded, for the same reason? When Vaughan writes "I saw eternity the other night / Like a great ring of pure and endless light," shall we say that he didn't *really* "see" it, so that the poem is not a visionary poem despite its own words? (I *will* "pass" on this one. It is not essential that we settle all problems in order to arrive at a useful definition of visionary poetry.)

The other side of the coin comes up when we turn from such questions as these and ask whether poems that are rich in concrete visual or perceptible images referring to the tangible everyday world thereby qualify as "visionary" because their perceptions are easily available to readers who have no special gifts and are granted no epiphanies—perceptions that are, therefore, in a sense public? "Prufrock"? Johnson's "London"? The descriptive poems often cited as products of the short-lived "Imagist" movement? (Once again, no, with no desire to "pass" this time: "seeing" that impresses us as neurotic in quality or satiric in intention does not tempt us to call it "visionary," though it may be salutary; and the presence of

the "visual" does not automatically make a poem "visionary.") Finally, what about "the poetry of meditation" when it
is rich in images drawn from our tangible public world, as it
often is, especially in the classic seventeenth-century examples? If such poetry affects us primarily through the power
of its images, should it not be called visionary? (Not if the
images seem called up by belief and are presented, in effect,
as illustrations.)

Visionary poetry so defined seems to be chiefly at least a
Romantic and post-Romantic phenomenon. Emerson, like
Blake before him, called for it but did not often write it.
Whitman is our first and greatest visionary poet, and Hart
Crane, Williams in his later work, Roethke beginning with
The Lost Son, Ammons, especially the early Ammons, and
David Wagoner in his later nature poems are others among
our American poetic visionaries.

This list is not intended to be inclusive, but it is deliberately exclusive, and of some of our finest poets. Dickinson
for instance usually seems too cerebral to be a visionary; she
analyzes and dissects. Frost in his nature poetry seems generally closer to Bryant than to Whitman. The early Stevens
seems to me an aesthete, the later Stevens a poetic philosopher; typically, in both phases, he either "imagines" or tries
to search out order and value, his "fictive music," where he
believes there is none. The images in his poetry are not about
the world but about ways of looking at the world: he is not
interested in real blackbirds. Stevens' fictive music is not just
"imagined" but "imaginary"—though late in life he seems to
have been trying to move beyond his solipsism, as in "An
Ordinary Evening in New Haven" and "Not Ideas About the
Thing but the Thing Itself." He was a major poet, but not, in
the terms I propose, a visionary poet.

Nor was Eliot. The early Eliot wrote brilliant poetry of alienation, the later Eliot, especially in *Four Quartets*, some of the finest poetry of religious meditation of our century—but, with the possible exception of a few passages in *The Four Quartets*, not what I would call visionary poetry. We may see the late poetry as reflecting the influence of Eliot's hard-won Christian faith without finding it essentially "visionary." Belief prepares us to see and plays a crucial role in our interpretation of what we see, but when belief seems central and in control, even when unstated, we lose the sense of discovery the visionary poem gives us. The visionary poet neither imagines the values he celebrates nor believes them into being but attentively and creatively perceives, discovers, or uncovers them. So they are finally not his but the world's, existing with or without his awareness of them.

Visionary poetry as I have come to think of it sees us as participants in the world, part and parcel of it, neither objective observers of it nor homeless in it. It thus runs counter to the poetry of alienation. It also runs counter to any sort of poetic "idealism" that would make whatever is valuable in the world the by-product of our minds. As I try to give specific content to such abstractions as these, my working assumption will be that there is no sharp and clear break between "sight" and "insight," "mind" and "matter," perceiver and perceived, thinking and seeing, subjective and objective. As Wittgenstein put it many years ago, "I must distinguish between the 'continuous seeing' of an aspect and the 'dawning' of an aspect. . . . The flashing of an aspect on us seems half visual experience, half thought."[1] Sight, insight,

1 Ludwig Wittgenstein, *Philosophical Investigations*, trans. G. E. M. Anscombe (3rd ed.; New York, n.d.), II, xi.

foresight, contemplation, prophecy, vision: even literal "seeing" is already "vision" and well on the way to becoming "visionary."

★   ★   ★

I have found support for my ideas in the books I have been told best reflect the results of current research in visual perception. In them, we read that photons of light entering the eye in inverted patterns enable us to see; but we never see photons, we see objects, by an act of interpretation. For example, R. L. Gregory writes:

The optical images in the eyes are but patterns of light: unimportant until used to read non-optical aspects of things. . . . Touch, taste and temperature senses must have developed before eyes: for visual patterns are only important when interpreted in terms of the world of objects. . . . As we shall see, eyes require intelligence to identify and locate objects in space, but intelligent brains could hardly have developed without eyes. It is not too much to say that eyes freed the nervous system from the tyranny of reflexes, leading to strategic planned behavior and ultimately to abstract thinking. . . . We not only believe what we see: to some extent we see what we believe. . . . All perception is theory-laden. . . . We need the power of symbols to extend our perceptual models of the world to cover cases beyond the range of direct experience.

And again:

There are many familiar so-called "ambiguous figures," which illustrate . . . how the same pattern of stimulation at the eye can give rise to different perceptions, and how the perception of objects goes beyond sensation. . . . Perception is not determined simply by the stimulus patterns; rather it is a dynamic searching for the best interpretation of the available data. . . . The senses do not give us a picture of the world directly; rather they provide evidence for the checking of hypotheses about what lies before us. Indeed, we may say that the perception of an object is an hypothesis, suggested and tested by the sensory data. . . . Perceiving and thinking are not independent: "I see what you mean" is not a puerile pun, but indicates a connection which is very real.

The author of the most recent book to come out of the vision laboratories is even more emphatic in his rejection of any simple mechanistic or photographic explanation of what goes on when we "see" something. John P. Frisby writes: "Attempts to explain seeing by building representations which simply mirror the outside world by some sort of physical equivalence" must be mistaken, for "seeing is a matter of building up *explicit symbolic description of the scene observed*. The photographic analogy is no good." Generally similar views, usually more cautiously expressed, may be found in Lloyd Kaufman's *Perception: The World Transformed*, and elsewhere.[2]

I have turned to such works as these rather than to Freud or Jung or their successors because I had an interest in keeping the "visionary" attached to waking experience of the "real," to what truly exists, whether we perceive it or not, to what is not "dreamed up," or first "imagined" and then "projected," or allowed to emerge from the Unconscious. Keeping it attached both to the body and the nervous system, and to the perceived world around us, seemed a way of doing that. I have no desire to belittle the contributions of either Freud or Jung to our understanding of human nature and

2 R. L. Gregory, *The Intelligent Eye* (New York, 1970), 12, 13, 15, 149; R. L. Gregory, *Eye and Brain* (3rd ed.; New York, 1978), 12, 13, 14; John P. Frisby, *Seeing: Illusion, Brain, and Mind* (New York, 1980), 25, 156 (the italics are the author's); Lloyd Kaufman, *Perception: The World Transformed* (New York, 1979), 173–82 and *passim*.

human experience, but I want to avoid "psychologism," one of the forms that solipsism is likely to take today.

We might expect such a "physicalistic" approach to yield a simple "realism" that would make it easy to distinguish illusion from reality, but when we check the conclusions of the vision researchers, we find that the objective-subjective ambiguities preserved in the language and apparent when we compare "eyesight" with "vision," and "vision" with "visionary," are not simply culturally, or philosophically, created but are in some sense built into nature, including our nature. Common sense and ordinary language encourage us to distinguish between "seeing" and "seeing *as*," but if the retinal image is "inherently ambiguous," as Frisby and the others tell us, where do we draw the line between the matter-of-fact and the metaphoric? If seeing even at the most literal level involves interpreting signals and perceiving relationships, then the metaphoric language of poetry need not be merely "emotive" or decorative, as the positivists would have it, lacking the "truth-value" of statements of fact, but noetic, meaningful—though of course the kind and degree of value it has as "truth" will be judged by each reader for himself.

Vision, literally as well as figuratively, is selective and purposive, allowing us to act, and is thus inevitably, unavoidably, both subjective and ambiguous—but it is still possible to talk meaningfully about visual illusions and peculiarly "ambiguous figures." For the sighted, "to attend to" and "to see" can perhaps not be distinguished in the laboratory, so that, in a very real sense, how we are able to "see" at all remains a mystery, but vision is an aid to survival only insofar as the object of our attention, or what we think we see, is really there and has the characteristics we think we perceive.

To be meaningful, and so useful to us, the "seen" must

be "seen *as*" by an act of mental interpretation, which need
not be conscious. (Culture and language do most of the interpreting for us most of the time. We are in no danger of
seeing a car as a tree.) But "seeing *as*" is at the heart of metaphoric language. It would seem then that the metaphors of
the poet give us the world as the poet sees it before, relating
perception and belief, he draws conclusions and "sees *that*."
Reading the poem, we find either that his metaphors have
revealed to us relationships we have not seen before, in which
case he has helped us to learn to see, or else, as perceptions
we cannot share, they remain his alone.

The ambiguities refuse to be dissolved, even in the vision laboratories. Visionary poets at any rate did not invent
them.

                         ★   ★   ★

I asked earlier how visionary poetry is related to the poetry
of meditation and to Imagist poetry. It is time to come back
to that question. The distinctions, as I see them, involve the
relations of seeing to thinking and believing (that is, the ter-
ritory explored in the vision laboratory), and of perceiver to
perceived (the realm of philosophy).

Meditative poetry. In the meditative poem, the object
(image) seems to be glanced at, or called to mind, and turned
into a "conceit" (many "Metaphysical" poems); or seen as
illustrative of a belief or generalization (Johnson's "London");
or looked at longer, reflected on, and used to draw lessons
from (Bryant's "To a Waterfowl"). Or the poem may begin
with reflection on a general subject like mortality or the state
of a culture, then turn to instances that support the thought.
Either way, thought or reflection shapes and dominates the
poem, and different illustrative images could be substituted.

Imagist poetry. The Imagist poet wishes to avoid the romantic, the sentimental, and the subjective, to be as "objective" in his way as the scientist is, or is thought to be, in his. His poem is meant to give the impression that he has looked carefully at the object, or at the image of it in his mind, and presented it as it really is, honestly, realistically, accurately, "objectively." The poem may describe the object in a straightforward, literal way (Williams' "Poem"), or metaphorically, in terms of other objects brought to mind by what has been seen (Pound's "In a Station at the Metro"). In either case, the poem is *descriptive*, and the thing or process seen or otherwise perceived appears to shape and dominate the poem. In either case also, a philosophic subject-object dualism is assumed, and perception is thought of as essentially passive or nonpurposive.

Visionary poetry. Like Imagist poetry, the visionary poem appears to begin in direct perception, not in reflection or thought. But unlike the Imagist poem, the visionary poem does not assume a dichotomy between the perceiver and the perceived, the poet and the image (as with Buber and the "I-It" way of knowing) or a clear unambiguous disjunction between perception and interpretation. It implies rather that responsible imaginative vision may be noetic, may disclose or uncover previously hidden aspects of being.

Metaphorically speaking, the visionary poet appears to have opened himself to the presence of what is, in all its "suchness," perceiving often not just visually but with all his senses (Roethke's "Night Journey"), letting it speak to him in its own terms and direct his reflections. Imaginative vision, interpretive perception, at once subjective and objective, purposive and open, seems to shape and dominate the poem (Whitman's "A Noiseless Patient Spider"). The image or images could not be changed to others to "illustrate" the same point.

For example, let us consider a meditative poem, Herbert's "Virtue":

> SWEET day, so cool, so calm, so bright!
> The bridal of the earth and sky—
> The dew shall weep thy fall to-night;
> For thou must die.
>
> Sweet rose, whose hue angry and brave
> Bids the rash gazer wipe his eye,
> Thy root is ever in its grave,
> And thou must die.
>
> Sweet Spring, full of sweet days and roses,
> A box where sweets compacted lie,
> My music shows ye have your closes,
> And all must die.
>
> Only a sweet and virtuous soul,
> Like season'd timber, never gives;
> But though the whole world turn to coal,
> Then chiefly lives.[3]

Herbert's poem is a short meditation in verse on time and eternity, this world and the next, in which the images seem more known than freshly seen, though the poem gains power because the "sweets" that must die are not dismissed or devalued but are all the dearer for their evanescence. The belief in personal immortality stated in the concluding stanza does not seem inevitably required by uninstructed experience of the day, the rose, and the spring; and other images of mortality might have been used.

I am speaking here of what we find in the poem. What may have prompted or inspired the poem is a different matter. Herbert may have looked long and lovingly at a rose on

3 *The New Oxford Book of English Verse*, ed. Helen Gardner (New York, 1972), 257.

a beautiful spring day, then have written the poem; but if perception is behind this poem, it still seems outside it.

Next, two poems from the "Imagist" movement, Pound's "In a Station at the Metro" and Williams' "Poem":

The apparition of these faces in the crowd;
Petals on a wet, black bough.

As the cat
climbed over
the top of

the jamcloset
first the right
forefoot

carefully
then the hind
stepped down

into the pit of
the empty
flowerpot[4]

Pound's "In a Station at the Metro" could be used to illustrate what Pound meant when he listed among the guiding principles of Imagism "direct treatment of the 'thing,' subjective or objective," if we read "direct" to mean "without comment." The speaker's perception is at once subjective (faces do not necessarily suggest flowers) and objective, or "objectivistic" (the faces have the reality only of an "apparition," and they suggest not persons but "things"—"petals"). The speaker's aesthetic response assumes the subject-object

4 Pound's poem is from *Selected Poems* (New York, 1949), 35; Williams' "Poem" is from *The Collected Earlier Poems* (New York, 1966), 340.

dualism of modern Western thought and leads to objectification.

Williams' "Poem" is objective in a different and deeper sense than Pound's. The speaker looks closely at the movements of the cat (no "apparition" to him) and describes what he sees empathically. ("Carefully" is not an instance of the "pathetic fallacy.") The concern with which details are perceived suggests that to the speaker the "thing"—the cat—has intrinsic value. But since this suggestion is not developed, the poem might be called "proto-visionary." (Williams would move beyond this poem later.)

Finally, three poems meant to illustrate what I have been saying about how I would like to see "visionary" used when applied to poetry, the first by Whitman, the pair of poems by Roethke. The poems have been chosen partly for their brevity. Better examples from Whitman would have been "Out of the Cradle" or "There Was a Child Went Forth" or any one of many sections of "Song of Myself." And Roethke's second poem may seem to move from the visionary to the meditative in its third line.

A Noiseless Patient Spider

A noiseless patient spider,
I mark'd where on a little promotory it stood
    isolated,
Mark'd how to explore the vacant vast surrounding,
It launch'd forth filament, filament, filament, out of
    itself,
Ever unreeling them, ever tirelessly speeding them.

And you O my soul where you stand,
Surrounded, detached, in measureless oceans of space,

Ceaselessly musing, venturing, throwing, seeking the
    spheres to connect them,
Till the bridge you will need be form'd, till the ductile
    anchor hold,
Till the gossamer thread you fling catch somewhere,
    O my soul.

Cuttings

Sticks-in-a-drowse droop over sugary loam,
Their intricate stem-fur dries;
But still the delicate slips keep coaxing up water;
The small cells bulge;

One nub of growth
Nudges a sand-crumb loose,
Pokes through a musty sheath
Its pale tendrilous horn.

Cuttings (later)

This urge, wrestle, resurrection of dry sticks,
Cut stems struggling to put down feet,
What saint strained so much,
Rose on such lopped limbs to a new life?

I can hear, underground, that sucking and sobbing,
In my veins, in my bones I feel it,—
The small waters seeping upward,
The tight grains parting at last.
When sprouts break out,
Slippery as fish,
I quail, lean to beginnings, sheath-wet.[5]

5   *The Collected Poems of Theodore Roethke* (New York, 1966), 37.

Whitman really looks at the spider and sees it freshly, not in terms of literary precedents or popular notions (spiders bite, and should be killed), finding it a living creature not unlike himself. In the second stanza he identifies himself with the spider, his spinning with its spinning, both needing to find something solid outside the self to anchor the web to. Although the poem seems to move from seeing to thinking in the second stanza, what has been seen is not forgotten: some other insect at work would *not* do as well. The poem illustrates what I meant when I spoke of the visionary poet's seeing us as participants. In this important respect it anticipates Roethke's two "Cuttings" poems.

The unity of being suggested by Whitman's analogy is concretely and powerfully felt in Roethke's poems. Nature is not "dead" or purposeless for Roethke, though the struggle of the living to survive is a touch-and-go affair. "Coaxing" and "nudges" do not strike me as examples of the "pathetic fallacy," though clearly the words describe purposive activity: we share organic chemistry, cellular biology, and the "instinct" to survive with the plants. But this placing of the human within nature does not "reduce" or lower the "saint" so much as lift the "sticks."

If the final lines of the second poem are read as having sexual suggestion, I take it to mean that the perception that began with the visual has become total, including the sense of touch and the kinesthetic senses: the speaker ends by "feeling with" the sticks that he began by seeing objectively as "out there," external to and unlike himself. If the seeing in these two poems has been in part made possible by Roethke's experience of greenhouses and a knowledge of organic biochemistry and the like, as we may suspect, it is also even more clearly an imaginative kind of seeing, not in any sense a stereotyping that would ignore the unexpected, the unprepared-for. Read together, the poems present an act of seeing that becomes an act of visionary knowing.

$$\star \quad \star \quad \star$$

As the preceding definitions and examples have implied, it would seem more acccurate to speak of visionary poems than of visionary poets. Blake and Yeats both created personally shaped mythologies, but only some, not all, of their poems should be called "visionary" if the preceding reflections have any validity. Emerson called for an American poet who would be a "Namer" and "Sayer" because he was first a "Seer" who would admit the world through his "transparent eyeball" and see its significance, but very few of his own poems move, as many of Whitman's and Roethke's do, from the literally visual to the metaphorically visionary. Whitman, our "visionary poet" if we have one, wrote many great visionary poems but also many poems of opinion and belief, including some that seem even more assertive than meditative. It would appear then that "visionary poetry" is in some sense a "style" of poetry, which a poet might consciously set out to write.

Yet it would seem not to be a "period style" in the sense in which Donne and Pope and Edward Taylor may be said to have written in period styles, "metaphysical" or "baroque" or "neoclassic." Although visionary poetry may well be a Romantic and post-Romantic phenomenon, it is certainly not the characteristic "period style" of either the last century or our own. Our century has seen all kinds of poetic styles tried out and discarded at an ever-accelerating pace. The creators of visionary poems in this century, particularly during the period of Modernism, have seemed to be swimming against the current, defying critical expectations. What gives twentieth-century poetry whatever unity it has does not seem to me to be a single "style" but a common outlook, for which "alienation" is perhaps as good a word as any. But my examples of visionary poems suggest the opposite of alienation.

The fact that visionary poems of the sort I have tried to define and illustrate have been written chiefly if not entirely in the past two centuries may perhaps best be understood in terms of intellectual and cultural history. In admittedly oversimplified shorthand terms, after the age of belief and the age of reason, poets—or some poets, sometimes—have felt it necessary to turn to personal, imaginative, subjective experience of the perceptible world itself, prior to prescribed interpretation, to the world of the senses ("nature"), and to try to find *there* the meanings they needed to live with and by. Williams' "no ideas but in things" can be applied to many of Wordsworth's poems almost as easily as to Williams' own, and with no difficulty at all to many of Whitman's or Roethke's.

I said earlier that I would like to delay comment on the philosophic implications equally of this approach to visionary poetry and of the visionary poems that have been my examples. It is time to come back to them, and I shall do so by way of two philosophically loaded statements by a current philosopher and a current scientist. First, the philosopher William Barrett, writing in his recent *The Illusion of Technique*: "The old comic strips used to show us truth dawning on one of their characters as an electric bulb lighting up in the head. These cartoonists seem to have gone to school with Descartes. . . . Nevertheless we should keep the image of light; only it is not an electric bulb flashing in our head when truth happens, but some portion of the world that has become illuminated."

Now, scientist Gregory Bateson concluding the main argument in his recent *Mind and Nature: A Necessary Unity:* "Chiaroscuro is all very well, but William Blake tells us firmly that wise men see outlines and therefore they draw them." [6]

In these statements, the philosopher and the scientist agree on two philosophic assumptions, neither of which is logically provable: nature is "real," not the by-product of mind; and nature is knowable.

"Wise men *see* outlines" because the outlines are there to be seen—though, to be sure, seeing them may require imagination, effort, insight as well as sight, even guesswork. If the choice still had to be made between philosophic "Realism" and "Idealism," this would be a modified version of Realism, but Realism is no more provable than Idealism, as Hume, Bishop Berkeley, and others have shown. Dr. Johnson kicked a real stone, not an idea of a stone, a fictive stone, or even a fabulated or metafictive stone. But kicking the stone "proved" nothing. The superiority of Realism over mentalistic Idealism is moral and aesthetic: moral because it puts a limit to man's tendency to see himself as the center of the universe and the source of all value; aesthetic because it encourages man to see things as they are, in their own right, in their unique suchness, not as his needs and their potential uses demand. To assume that a tree, a mountain, a fish, or a rock is less "real" than my perception of it is both morally revolting and aesthetically stultifying: to deny it "reality" is at once to deny it value and to be unable to see it as it is.

"Some portion of the world has become illuminated." If so, nature must be not only there to be known but *knowable.* It is often pointed out that this is an assumption made by

6   William Barrett, *The Illusion of Technique* (New York, 1978), 143; Gregory Bateson, *Mind and Nature: A Necessary Unity* (New York, 1979), 202.

scientists, an act of faith necessary to their work. It is, but it is also an assumption acted on by all of us constantly in our daily lives, or we would not survive. Even in practical matters, knowledge must often be achieved by effort, creative effort, with "facts," memories, expectations, inferences, and dubious interpretations mixed together to serve as our only basis for a decision. It is becoming fashionable to call knowledge a "construct," which it is, but not a construct spun out of the mind alone. Even Whitman's spider, spinning the filament out of itself, needed a base to start from and something solid to attach the free end to.

To see nature as totally unknowable, so that fictions and fabulations are all we have, is to let the fear of being taken in or found naïve control us. Skepticism of this sort, currently popular, may appear to be the only way left us of defending the importance of literature and myth, but what is thus defended is first emptied of significance. The problem of appearance and reality would not have engaged thinkers through the ages had it not been assumed that it is worthwhile to try to distinguish them. We act on that assumption, that faith, hour by hour every day. The alternative is to embrace irrationality and rename it "reason."

The philosopher and the scientist agree, too, elsewhere in their books if not clearly in these statements, in rejecting any sharp discontinuity between mind and matter (compare the purposive or "teleological" behavior of the "sticks" in Roethke's poems) and between man and nature (compare Whitman and his spider). Barrett finds our century's analytic philosophy at a dead end and an act of faith necessary for the "will to believe" and to live. Bateson's neonaturalism leaves room for experience of the sacred. For neither writer does nature bear any resemblance at all to Stevens' "Snow Man." As the scientist-philosopher C. F. von Weizsäcker has re-

cently argued in *The Unity of Nature*, the uncertainty principle has rendered the contrast between philosophic Realism
and Idealism meaningless.[7] Here, as in both Barrett's and
Bateson's books, we are well beyond both Descartian dualism and the nineteenth century's positivistic ("realistic") interpretation of science—at last, as Whitehead already was in
his *Science and the Modern World* in 1925.

And as the visionary poets have been all along, without
being either scientists or philosophers, and without necessarily having to create personal myths as Blake and Yeats did.
At his best, Whitman did not philosophize, theologize, or
mythologize: he trusted his senses, his intuitions, and his
body. When "the terrible doubt of appearances" troubled
him, he could be reassured of the "reality" of the world he
perceived by the touch of a comrade's hand or the smell of a
salt marsh.

If, as I think, Barrett and Bateson speak not only from
but for this apocalyptic time of ours—when for many the self
has come to seem as unreal, as merely "fictive," as the patterns of humanly relevant meaning once found in nature came
to seem a century or so ago—then, so far as philosophic
thought is concerned, we may be moving into an age when
visionary poems will not be so rare as they have been since
Blake first called for them. If this should prove to be so, it
would be a cause for hope in a time when reasons for hope
are not easy to come by. For visionary poems can help us to
see better, in greater depth, and in more humanly meaningful
patterns of order.

★   ★   ★

My first book, *The Heel of Elohim: Science and Values in Mod-*

7   *The Unity of Nature*, trans. Francis J. Zucker (New York, 1980), *passim*.

ern American Poetry (1950) was dedicated in this way: "To
Louise, Veronica, and Jane, who daily remind me that values
are imbedded in the nature of things"—not in the mind only,
or in our wishes (or even in the hypothetical "collective unconscious"), but in "things." "No ideas but in things" has
often been understood as implying a reductive positivism, as
though our knowledge were not a construct as well as a discovery. (Our "constructs" enable us to "discover.") Or it has
been thought to mean that only "material" things are "real."

But it seems to me it would be just as reasonable to see
the phrase as pointing toward the idea of our participation in
a mysterious on-going reality in which meaning and value
are intrinsic, as Williams himself seems to be doing in "A
Unison," or as Roethke does in "Cuttings" and "Cuttings
(later)." Much of what has been called "the pathetic fallacy"
strikes me as neither pathetic nor a fallacy. Whitehead dis-
posed of the "alien universe" and "dead nature" notions a half
century ago, though critics for whom Stevens is still the ex-
emplar of contemporary poetic vision seem not to know it.
Life is precarious, survival is threatened—as it is in "Cuttings"—and hope for our children is difficult to maintain, but
a sick culture that offers no support and brings its poets to
breakdown or suicide is at least as much to blame as "the
nature of things," which may be tragic—if not for the young,
certainly for the aging—but is not necessarily meaningless,
absurd, or pointless. To the extent that what follows is per-
suasive, it will appear that poets when they write visionary
poems are neither dreaming up fictive music nor projecting
neurotic tensions but are perceiving in depth what is "out
there," beyond the conscious mind and the self, but also in
the body and brain, using the senses and imaginative intelligence as means of discovery.

CHAPTER II

Walt Whitman

"I and the Old Round Earth"

*Who knows the curious mystery of the eyesight? The other senses cor-
roborate themselves, but this is removed from any proof but its own and
foreruns the identities of the spiritual world.*
            —1855 Preface

*As he [the poet] sees the farthest he has the most faith. His thoughts
are the hymns of the praise of things. In the talk on the soul and eternity
and God off of his equal plane he is silent. . . . He sees eternity in men
and women. . . . He does not see men and women as dreams or dots.*
            —1855 Preface

*There is, in sanest hours, a consciousness, a thought that rises, indepen-
dent, lifted out from all else, calm, like the stars, shining eternal. This is
the thought of identity, yours for you, whoever you are, as mine for
me. . . . Under the luminousness of real vision, it alone takes possession,
takes value.*
            —"Democratic Vistas"

Our greatest poet was also our greatest visionary poet—*visionary*, American style: loosely empiricist, in the sense of subjecting received beliefs to the test of personal experience, and more sensuous, intuitive, and practical than logical. Students of American philosophy and American religion have found comparable emphases in their subjects.

There are of course other senses of *visionary*, especially the one we are likely to have in mind when we apply the word to Blake, the prototypical visionary poet. If we have Blake in mind, *visionary* points less to sense perception and concentration on personal experience than to free imagination working to restructure conventionally accepted beliefs and values, and ultimately to the creation of new myths allegorically expressed. The visionary poet in this sense dreams of a better world to come, in this life or the next, and rejects what he finds false and wrong in this one. Thus Blake could write that "the Nature of my Work is Visionary or Imaginative; it is an Endeavor to Restore . . . the Golden Age." When *visionary* carries this meaning, it is appropriate to speak, as his interpreters have, of Blake's "visionary politics" and "visionary myth-making." Blake and Whitman have much in common, but Whitman created no new mythology of the sort we find in Blake's prophetic books.

Still another kind of "visionary poet" would be the "blind Seer" described by Milton in the Invocation to Book III of *Paradise Lost*, when he prays that he may be able to "see and tell / Of things invisible to mortal sight," his mind illuminated by a "Celestial light" despite his blindness. But the linguistic root of *visionary* is *vision*—that is, one of the senses—so that *vision* in Milton's sense becomes wholly metaphoric: seeing, as it were, with the eye, as it were, of faith, through the lenses of memory and belief. This traditional sense of *visionary* seems to describe Whitman's poetic impulse and achievement in his finest poems only very partially and imperfectly, though it fits some of his late visionary poems well enough. In the poems of his most creative period, though the "seeing" requires an act of faith, the faith is still tied to the literally perceptible as its ground.

In his own fashion, Whitman was as religious a poet as Milton and Blake before him. Early and late, he thought of his Book as a "new Bible" that would help future readers to live well and have faith in themselves and in life. But if it were to have this effect, he thought it would not be by the cogency of its reinterpretations of the received biblical myths but by its power to move his readers to feel that the saving Word was waiting to be personally discovered in the grass and the earth beneath their feet, in the world around them and in their own bodies. Milton had interpreted Scripture, in a somewhat heterodox way perhaps but faithfully, as he thought. Blake had radically reinterpreted and supplemented it. Whitman simply "accepted" it, along with other Sacred Books, without any concern for theological clarity. His Christ could be "dead and divine and brother of all," all at once. Blake, with the Deists in mind, rejected the possibility of a "natural Religion," but "natural religion" in a less rationalistic sense than the one Blake had in mind is precisely what lies at the center of Whitman's work. This is presumably one of the reasons why his poems are so very different from Blake's, even when their thematic implications can be seen as overlapping.

To be sure, if our interest is chiefly in the abstract thought of the two poets, it is easy enough to find parallels between them, with Blake anticipating Whitman—and much of the rest of modern poetry—in many important ways, in rejecting "Puritanism," for instance, and in emphasizing the prophetic role of imaginative vision. But the radical differences between their poems cannot be accounted for by any talk about the differences between period styles. Blake, for instance, anticipated Whitman in writing a prophetic poem about America, but Whitman, deeply concerned about his country's future as he was, never wrote any poem that even remotely resembles Blake's *America a Prophecy*. One of the reasons, I should suppose, is that, while for Blake poetic "Vision" was synonymous with both "Prophecy" and "Imagination," the meaning Whitman attached to "vision" never, even in the least sensuous and imaginative poems of his decline, totally lost its connection with sight, with literal seeing. This may be why Whitman's most personal poems seem more truly prophetic than those like "Passage to India" in which he consciously adopted the role of poet-prophet. Again and again in the poems of personal experience he suggests the direction of Whitehead's thought in *Process and Reality*, and his mental picture of the earth anticipated the photographs we have seen of the planet taken from space, but his *ideas* often seem simply those of his own time. What is prophetic in his poems rests on perception, feeling, and imaginative vision, not on clear logical thinking.

Ideas that seem strikingly similar in the two poets result in very different poetry. "The world of Imagination," Blake could say, "is the world of Eternity." Whitman's concern with the eternal was probably at least as strong as Blake's, but if he had undertaken to revise Blake's statement he might have written, "the world of the imagination is 'the old round earth,'" which, he felt sure, would be more than enough to supply the true poet with suggestions of the eternal. But he found the earth too various to be reduced to systematic allegory. Any "myth" to be found in his work thus remains comparatively raw, crude, impure, mixed with stubborn lumps of biography impossible to fit into any coherent system of thought—hardly more, really, than what he once called "hints and guesses" derived from his situation and his ideal self-image. But the resulting systematic deficiency in his work is a poetic deficiency only if we read poetry as versified philosophy. As Mark Schorer was the first to say, a Whitman undisturbed by his own philosophic and theological contradictions was "free to direct his observation to the objects of the external world with stricter concentration than Blake."[1]

So, it seems to me, even when Whitman seems closest to Blake as a visionary, there is almost always at least a subtle difference in what is meant by "vision." When Blake, for instance, seems to be announcing a central aspect of Whitman's program by writing, "to see the World in a grain of sand . . . and Eternity in an hour," the meaning is not quite the same as that in Whitman's late poem, "Grand Is the Seen," which both reminds us of Blake by deciding that the "Unseen," like Blake's "Eternity," is still "grander," and remains good Whitman by making "unseen" derive its meaning from its contrast with the literally, visually "seen." The shade of difference here becomes clearer if we compare what "seeing" means, and how it works, in Blake's "Introduction" to "Songs of Innocence" ("On a cloud I saw a child") with the predominantly visual imagery in Whitman's "There Was a Child Went Forth." Blake's child is at all times a generalized symbol of childhood, Whitman's first of all a particular literal child, himself, and only then, when the total poem has had its effect, symbolic of the process of growth, maturation, and realized potential.

Both Whitman and Blake, of course, saw the true poet as having a prophetic function, but even while sharing this

1 Mark Schorer, *William Blake: The Politics of Vision* (New York, 1946), 314.

common Romantic idea they differed on *how* the poet could be a prophet. Blake, for instance, in his "Introduction" to "Songs of Experience" writes of the seeing and hearing a poet-prophet does in this way:

> Hear the voice of the Bard!
> Who Present, Past, & Future sees
> Whose ears have heard,
> The Holy Word,
> That walk'd among the ancient trees.

But Whitman, writing in a similarly prophetic vein, begins his chief programmatic poems simply with

> Starting from fish-shape Paumanok where I was born

and

> I celebrate myself, and sing myself
> And what I assume you shall assume.

Different religious and cultural backgrounds as well as different personalities are revealed in this contrast, of course, but that is not all. There is a difference in the way the two poets conceive of what it means to see and hear the Holy Word, a difference that becomes apparent when we compare Blake's "London" with, for example, section 8 of "Song of Myself." Both poems concentrate on what the poet says he has seen and heard. In Blake's poem, surely one of his loveliest, the imagery is generalized: what is "seen" in the poem is seen as evidence, instances of social injustice. "I wander thro' each chartered street," the poet tells us,

> And mark in every face I meet
> Marks of weakness, marks of woe.

What Whitman sees is very different:

> The little one sleeps in its cradle,
> I lift the gauze and look a long time, and silently
>   brush away flies with my hand.

> The youngster and the red-faced girl turn aside up
>   the bushy hill,
> I peeringly view them from the top.

Blake's "marking" the signs of the distress of the London poor seems the work of "the mind's eye," of thought and conscience. Blake's "mark" and Whitman's "mind" as he concludes the section appear to have very similar meanings, but when Whitman says "I mind them," "mind" means first of all "observe attentively," and only then, because such attention implies sympathetic concern, "care about." Tying his "vision" to the empirical, the perceptibly concrete, Whitman initiated one of the distinguishing features of later American visionary poetry.

★   ★   ★

In this respect Whitman seems to me closer to the early Wordsworth than to Blake. To be sure, he was no "nature poet" like Wordsworth, but a poet of the city like Blake, but we make too much of this difference if we forget what Whitehead wrote long ago in *Science and the Modern World* of the significance of the turn to nature of Wordsworth and his contemporaries—that "the nature-poetry of the romantic revival was a protest on behalf of the organic view of nature, and also a protest against the exclusion of value from the essence of matter of fact."[2] Whitman's "intimations" perhaps came more often in company than in solitude, but this and other obvious differences should not blind us to what he and Wordsworth have in common.

2 Alfred North Whitehead, *Science and the Modern World* (New York, 1931), 138.

Most important perhaps is the fact that the self and its growth are so often both subject and theme of the two poets. Both men turn away from myth, classical or religious, and from allegory to a kind of "realism," but the "realism" that marks their poetry is not that of a neutral observer but might be described as "the self's response to the world." No "mind and matter" disjunction is implied in this description: neither "self" nor "world" can be imagined alone, in separation from the other. If we are thinking in philosophic terms, as Whitehead was in the quotation above, we might say that the world within the mind is blended with the world outside the mind in the work of both poets, so that their "realism" may be called "subjective."

But from this we should not conclude, as some of Whitman's critics have, that Whitman's world is either simply "projected" out of the self or else sucked into the hungry self to lose all its independent reality. Such metaphors rest on and are prompted by a naïve mind-matter, self-world dichotomy and inevitably lead to a misreading of the poetry. "There Was a Child Went Forth" and the opening sections of *The Prelude*, for instance, both describe "realistically" what the mature poet saw as having influenced him in childhood, and both poems have as their ultimate subjects the "growth of a poet's mind"—the subtitle of Wordsworth's poem. Wordsworth's speculations on how "the growing faculties of sense" that make the mind "creator and receiver both, / Working but in alliance with the works / Which it beholds" certainly *sound* like no lines of Whitman's we have ever read—though the thought is common to both poets—but Whitman might have said about many of his own early poems what Wordsworth said of one of his, that "there is not an image in it which I have not observed. . . . I was an eye-witness of this."

And he might well have spoken as Wordsworth did of

his "consciousness of the infinite variety of natural appearances which had been unnoticed" by the poets before him, as he might also have said with Wordsworth that in picturing the world as he did he had "consulted nature and [his] feelings"—though to be sure "nature" in such a statement would have had a more inclusive meaning for him than it had for Wordsworth. For both poets sense experience was central, the starting point of speculation and hope. Whitman's analogue of Wordsworth's purely descriptive passages are his so-called "catalogues," a term that seems to omit the element of subjectivity implicit in the lists.

For both poets, in short, what Wordsworth once called "the ocular spectrum" of the simply "out there" was tempered and balanced by what could be seen only with the aid of what Wordsworth, once again, called "the inward eye," so that, though both poets were engaged in an attempt to "see into the life of things" (still Wordsworth's words), neither felt any confidence in the unfettered imagination. In this respect they stand in contrast with Blake, whose reliance on the constructive imagination grew with the years. Thus Blake may be read as anticipating Stevens, while the early Wordsworth and Whitman point rather in the direction of Williams. No "order" that could be found only in art, at Key West or elsewhere, would have satisfied either poet. Those passages in the later books of *The Prelude* that elevate mind above nature and thus may seem to point more to Stevens than to Whitman should be read with the understanding that for both early and late Wordsworth, "mind" carried a religious, not a secular, meaning, connoting the immanence of the divine, or "spirit."

To say this is not to overlook the enormous differences between the two. Whitman was never a solitary "worshiper of nature," and he cannot be imagined choosing as his subjects for a poem "Guilt and Sorrow," as Wordsworth once did in a little-known work. He preferred not to write about the "mystery . . . and the heavy weight of all this unintelligible world" that so often left Wordsworth in "a sad perplexity," but the mystery and the weight nevertheless lie behind many of his best poems.

★   ★   ★

As a visionary poet, Whitman lived and wrote midway between the age of Blake and Wordsworth and that of Stevens, who thought that "the greatest poverty is not to live / In a physical world." Whitman sought the Logos not in Prophetic Vision as Blake conceived it, seeing a child on a cloud or an angel in a tree, or in the play of aesthetic Imagination, which could create a fictive music to counter a threatening Reality, as Stevens later would, but in sensuous experience and sense perception. What seems philosophic naïveté and a new poetic vision are both to be found in a sentence already alluded to written into his copy of the 1860 edition and intended for a revision of the poem then called "To the Sayers of Words" (later entitled "Song of the Rolling Earth"): "This rolling earth is the word to be said."[3] Expanded in the poem as it appears in the Deathbed Edition, the idea would be spelled out more fully: "The substantial words are in the ground and sea, / They are in the air, they are in you." This in a poem addressed to poets, advising them to cultivate the innocent eye and trust it. Seeming to ignore the effect of past experience and existing ideas on present perception, the need to interpret in order to see, and the need for verbal symbols if we are to express what we see, the passage may well strike us

3 See *Walt Whitman's Blue Book: The 1860–61 Leaves of Grass Containing His Manuscript Additions and Revisions*, ed. Arthur Golden (2 vols.; New York, 1968), I, iii, 329, II, 329.

as expressing a naïve faith unavailable to us today, though certain passages in Heidegger and the later Wittgenstein may be read as offering philosophic support for Whitman's intuitive metaphors.

Yet it was just this faith that shaped and found expression in many of Whitman's greatest poems. His visionary triumphs never seriously or for long question the faith that, when we perceive in depth, we "see"—as Blake thought we should—the infinite hidden within the finite, the world of spirit incarnate in space and time. If the affirmations in such poems as "There Was a Child Went Forth," "Crossing Brooklyn Ferry," "Song of Myself," and "Out of the Cradle Endlessly Rocking" (earlier called, we may note, "A Word out of the Sea") do not seem too easily achieved to be taken seriously, the reason is surely not that they probe the hard epistemological problems and solve them philosophically to our satisfaction.

Yet all these greatest expressions of Whitman's visionary faith were written by 1860—or, if we should add "When Lilacs Last in the Dooryard Bloom'd" to them, by 1865-'66. After that, a more thoughtful—or perhaps just less confident and creative?—poet, more acutely aware of the subjective and constructive aspects of vision, of the interdependence of seeing and believing, of the possibility of optical illusions and of the fact that the earth does not automatically supply the word needed for its interpretation, generally wrote both more self-consciously in the role of Poet-Prophet, and less memorably. In the sixties and later, the visionary faith expressed in the earlier great poems became intermittent, impossible to sustain for a long poem—again perhaps with the exception of "Lilacs," Whitman's last wholly great long poem, and even there the final affirmation may seem more the achievement of art than the expression of faith, if such a distinction has any meaning. The visual still suffices as the base for the visionary in such short poems of the early sixties as "Cavalry Crossing a Ford," "A Sight in Camp in the Daybreak Gray and Dim," "When I Heard the Learn'd Astronomer," "A Noiseless Patient Spider," and others, but the vision in such poems does not make any explicit, or even implicit, claim to being Prophecy. When in these years Whitman did write in a consciously Prophetic-Visionary role, he produced the flawed visionary poem "Passage to India," in which an ambitious design is undercut again and again by a failure of vision. After that, we have "The Mystic Trumpeter," "Sparkles from the Wheel," and a few other poems in which the visionary is related in one·way or another to the concretely perceptible, but for the most part the late poems at their best express an abstractly visionary wisdom that has become largely independent of the senses, as it is in "As I Watch'd the Ploughman Ploughing," in which the plowman and the harvester are as much generic figures as Blake's child on a cloud. "I Sit and Look Out" might almost be described as a poem about why he can't write a visionary poem about what he sees and hears—"I sit and look out. . . . See, hear, and am silent."

★   ★   ★

I have called attention to what must seem to us the philosophically too-simple faith in the reports of the senses that characterized Whitman's great early visionary poems, but it would be a mistake to suppose that this faith was the gift simply of youthful vigor and lack of thought, a faith never threatened, never challenged by any skepticism. It was an achievement, rather, cultivated and carefully nourished even then, as three poems of the period may serve to illustrate.

"Faces," dating from 1855, might well be called Whitman's "ambiguous figures" poem—to borrow a phrase from today's experimenters in the vision laboratories. "How shall these faces be seen?" is the unstated question that the poem ponders and attempts to answer. Seeing faces both ugly and handsome, expressive and blank, in such a way that he can be "content" with them all depends, as he says, on his believing in their potential, their continuity in growth. Without that assumption, in section 2 he sees only ugly, evil, and dying faces and hears "an unceasing death-bell." But this faithless vision is a "trick," he decides in section 3, a trick that he will not be taken in by. Even the "smear'd and slobbering idiot they had at the asylum. . . . my brother" is potentially, "in a score or two of ages," "perfect and unharmed, every inch as good as myself." Seeing the present truly, then, requires assuming a future. As he had said in his preface, the poet "sees eternity in men and women" because he "sees the farthest."[4]

Section 4, opening with "The Lord advances, and yet advances," holding out a hand, is the turning point in the poem.

> Out of this face emerge banners and horses—
> O superb! I see what is coming,
> ....
> I hear victorious drums.

This face rescues the poet, making it possible now to see all the former actual faces as resembling that of "the Master himself" and to "read the promise and patiently wait." The sec-

4 In "Faces" and elsewhere, Whitman anticipates aspects of Whitehead's thought in *Process and Reality*. See "possibility" in the index of Alfred North Whitehead, *Process and Reality: Corrected Edition*, ed. Griffin and Sherburne (New York, 1978).

tion ends with dreamlike imagery as the face becomes a flower, then feminine, then a voice calling out to be filled with honey and touched, bent down to, rubbed. Sight here gives way to more primitive senses less easy to doubt, less in need of interpretation. The result, in the final section of the poem, is that the speaker sees the "old face of the mother of many children" and is at last "fully content" with what he sees. The old woman as he sees her seems to give perfect expression to "the melodious character of the earth." The sight of her takes him, he says, "beyond" philosophy to where he is no longer troubled by the faces that refuse to fit into his conception of reality. The poem could not possibly be described as intellectually naïve, but the guarantor of true vision, we note, is a product neither of the logical nor of the allegorizing mind. If section 4 needs "explaining" by being fitted into an intellectual scheme—as it seems to me not to— then a reading in terms of Jungian archetypes could account for some features, a Christian reading for others. But the poem is clear enough without either superstructure. The troubled speaker in the end has simply been helped to see the "real" truly by an envisioned, imagined face and a hand reached out to touch his. The visual has found its meaning in its relation to the visionary.

Another 1855 poem that may be cited as evidence that Whitman's early faith in the reports of his senses was not the result of lack of awareness of or reflection on the human situation is "To Think of Time," which is not, formally or structurally, a visionary poem but a poetic meditation on mortality and the central core belief of Whitman's visionary affirmation, immortality. "Have you guess'd you yourself would not continue / Have you dreaded these earth-beetles?" If not, then reflection will tell you that "Not a day passes, not a minute or second without a corpse. . . . / Slow-moving and black lines creep over the whole earth—they never cease—they are the burial lines." Death is "the vulgar fate," but "what will be will be well, for what is is well." No reason is given for this confidence beyond the fact that "I have dream'd that the purpose and essence of the known life, the transient, / Is to form and decide identity for the unknown life, the permanent." For "evidence" we have only the speaker's admission of need:

> Do you suspect death? If I were to suspect death I should
> die now,

> Do you think I could walk pleasantly and well-suited
> toward annihilation?

The unavoidable objective-subjective ambiguity of vision, the necessity of "imagining" and "interpreting" in order to "see," is as central in this poem as it is in "Faces," though here it is less recreated than talked about in the poem as a whole. Section 4 presents a "sample of the life and death" of a workman in the form of a "reminiscence" that is quite specific and sometimes concretely visual—"Cold dash of waves at the ferry-wharf, posh and ice in the river, half-frozen mud in the streets, / A gray discouraged sky overhead." But section 8, in which the dream is offered as countering the dread, is wholly generalized except in the lines devoted to death, which are somewhat more concretely imagistic:

If all came but to ashes of dung,
If maggots and rats ended us, then Alarum! for we are betrayed,
Then indeed suspicion of death.

In this poem, then, what can be seen and what is "dream'd"—and in some sense believed—remain in conflict, and insofar as any resolution of the conflict is offered, it is asserted in defiance of logic:

> I swear I think now that every thing without exception has
>   an eternal soul!
> The trees have, rooted in the ground! the weeds of the sea
>   have! the animals!
> I swear I think there is nothing but immortality!

By the end of the poem, the reports of the senses have
been not so much reinterpreted as overruled. What appears
to be is not what is. But that is not the way Whitman's great
visionary poems work. There, appearance is normally ambiguous and sometimes threatening, but it is not finally at
odds with reality.

The possibility that the phenomenal world of the senses
may tell us nothing at all of the real and the permanent is the
explicit subject of another meditative poem on the nature of
vision, "Of the Terrible Doubt of Appearances," which first
appeared in the 1860 edition. The problem behind the poem
is a philosophic one, the epistemological skepticism which,
as Whitman undoubtedly knew, Emerson had treated in the
essays "Experience" and "Illusions," after the heartening effect of the metaphysical Idealism espoused in the early "Nature" had diminished. If Nature is a product of mind, even of
individual minds, how can it offer any guarantee of the truth
of our ideas? Subjectivity has this price tag on it.

Whitman gives Emerson's problem specific personal dimensions in his opening lines:

> Of the terrible doubt of appearances,
> Of the uncertainty after all, that we may be deluded,
> That may-be reliance and hope are but speculations after all,
> That may-be identity beyond the grave is a beautiful fable only,
> May-be the things I perceive, the animals, plants, men, hills,
>   shining and flowing waters,
> The skies of day and night, colors, densities, forms, may-be

these are (as doubtless they are) only apparitions, and the
real something has yet to be known, . . .

But his "solution" is not Emerson's: neither patience (as at
the end of "Experience") nor direct communion with the
gods hidden behind appearances—in effect apprehension of
the "spiritual laws" (as at the end of "Illusions")—puts such
doubts to rest for Whitman, but love, physically expressed
and so available to the senses, does:

> To me these and the like of these are curiously answer'd by
>   my lovers, my dear friends,
> When he whom I love travels with me or sits a long while
>   holding me by the hand,
> When subtle air, the impalpable, the sense that words and
>   reason hold not, surround us and pervade us,
> Then I am charged with untold and untellable wisdom, I am
>   silent, I require nothing further,
> I cannot answer the question of appearances or that of identity
>   beyond the grave,
> But I walk or sit indifferent, I am satisfied,
> He ahold of my hand has completely satisfied me.

    Whitman's religious faith then in himself and in the real
and lasting value of the perceived world was challenged early
and hard both by what has always challenged man's faith,
"the problem of evil," including the suffering of the innocent
and the fear of death, and by the skepticism potential in
Emerson's version of subjective Idealism. Whitman's response to these challenges was certainly not logical, not even,
we might say, deeply thoughtful, but not less satisfying
therefore.

★   ★   ★

All the different kinds of "vision" that may be found in Whitman's visionary poems appear very early: he did not begin as one kind of visionary and end, after a clear and steady development, as another. Yet, when we compare the 1855 edition with those published after the Civil War, a general tendency to move from the literal to the figurative meanings of "vision" may be noted in the poems in which images are central to the poem's movement. If this development had been steady and clear, as it was not, we might schematize it by saying that the poems move from eyesight to illuminated vision to prophetic envisaging to generalized belief, and note that this movement coincides with Whitman's declining power as a poet, but that is a partial truth, a partial distortion, it seems to me.

Still, it is true that all but one of Whitman's greatest visionary poems—the exception being "When Lilacs Last in the Dooryard Bloom'd"—were completed before 1860, and all of them exhibit a tension between the literal and the figurative meanings of vision, between sight and insight, seeing and interpreting, the "real" and the "imagined," objective and subjective. That Whitman's visionary triumphs may be so characterized will seem more plausible, I hope, if the poems I have in mind are first contrasted with two early and two late poems that deserve, or demand, to be called "visionary" but do not exhibit in the same degree the tension I have attributed to the "triumphs."

Despite the fact that "I Sing the Body Electric" celebrates the body and physical health rather than visionary experience as we usually think of it, the poem is "visionary" from several points of view. In the first place, the imagery in the poem is predominantly visual, though the other senses by which we make contact with the world outside the mind, particularly the kinesthetic or "body-feeling," are acknowledged. To celebrate the body is, by implication, to give importance to the senses, of which eyesight is only one. Then, too, since from the standpoint of consciousness the body is "a peculiarly intimate bit of the world"—as Whitehead has reminded us[5]—the thrust of the poem is that characteristic of visionary poetry generally, toward uniting "mind" and "matter" or "nature" and thus narrowing the Descartean gulf between the two, between perceiver and perceived.

Finally, of course, the "prophetic" aspect of visionary poetry may be found in the poem, too. Whitman did not intend this poem to be "prophetic" in the way he intended "Passage to India" to be, but history has proved it so: it points beyond Whitman's time and toward ours in too many ways to enumerate, not all of them necessarily healthy, toward our how-to sex manuals and our narcissism as well as toward new concepts of mind-body unity. But whatever distortions we may have introduced into Whitman's vision, when we remember the date the poem was written we must call it prophetic-visionary: "A man's body at auction, / . . . . Gentlemen look on this wonder, / . . . . Flakes of breast-muscle, pliant backbone and neck, flesh not flabby, good-sized arms and legs, / . . . . If any thing is sacred the human body is sacred. . . . / There is something in staying close to men and women and looking on them, and in the contact and odor of them, that pleases the soul well."

But seeing and otherwise sensing the body as "sacred," and not just pleasing, may seem too easily achieved, may seem not to require any effort. After all, the flesh of the aged *is* generally "flabby" and the legs of the undernourished are not likely to be "good-sized." There is nothing to oppose the visionary thrust of the poem, so that when we read "I see my

5 "For the organic theory, the most primitive perception is 'feeling the body as functioning.' . . . The body, however, is only a peculiarly intimate bit of the world." Whitehead, *Process and Reality*, 81.

soul reflected in Nature" we may well wonder why and how. Which aspect of "Nature" best reflects the soul? Is such visionary seeing-feeling the result simply of good health? In the greater poems, the visionary affirmation is achieved, not assumed and asserted.

"The Sleepers"—"I wander all night in my vision"—is surely one of Whitman's most impressive poems, but it seems, in the body of Whitman's work, a special case: vision, at once concrete and meaningful, is not achieved but granted in a dream. The speaker has no more need of ordinary eyesight after the dreaming is begun: "Now I pierce the darkness, new beings appear, / The earth recedes from me into the night, / I saw that it was beautiful, and I see that what is not the earth is beautiful." Drawing on the "dream-power" that Emerson had attributed to the poet he hoped for, the speaker is granted what amounts to a Revelation as he wanders "confused, lost . . . gazing." The poem that results is one of Whitman's finest but not, as I see it, characteristic of his work. Normally, there was no need for the earth to recede into darkness for Whitman to find it beautiful.

At the opposite end of the spectrum of Whitman's visionary poetry is "I Sit and Look Out," first printed in the 1860 edition. Like "The Sleepers," it may be called a visionary poem, yet it does not reenact the special kind of seeing that makes the visionary triumphs peculiarly Whitman's own, without precedent in earlier poetry. Nine of this poem's ten lines contain *see* or a synonym as the operative verb, with *hear* substituting for it in the exceptional tenth.

But what is "seen" is nothing specific, nothing that can be visualized concretely. "Vision" in the poem is the product of thoughtful interpretation of experience, colored by the dark mood induced by the outbreak of the war. I find the poem ·a moving and memorable one that presents an awareness of the constancy of pain and suffering that makes the assertion in "Starting From Paumanok" that "I say there is in fact no evil" seem desperately willed, immature, and hollow; but the greater wisdom of the later poem does not make it a poem we can imagine only Whitman having written. What does that is the way all but the last two lines begin with "I" and the way all of them move with verbs denoting perception, though now they carry only a figurative meaning, calling up the generalized results of particular perceptions. Fortunately for the power of the poem, Whitman does not try to tell us how what he has seen and heard "has reference to the soul":

I sit and look out upon all the sorrows of the world,
    and upon all oppression and shame.
I hear secret convulsive sobs from young men at anguish with
    themselves, remorseful after deeds done,
I see in low life the mother misused by her children, dying
    neglected, gaunt, desperate,
I see the wife misused by her husband, I see the treacherous
    seducer of young women,
I mark the ranklings of jealousy and unrequited love attempted
    to be hid, I see these sights on the earth,
I see the workings of battle, pestilence, tyranny, I see martyrs
    and prisoners,
I observe a famine at sea, I observe the sailors casting lots
    who shall be kill'd to preserve the lives of the rest,
I observe the slights and degradations cast by arrogant persons
    upon laborers, the poor, and upon negroes, and the like;
All these—all the meanness and agony without end I sitting
    look out upon,
See, hear, and am silent.

★   ★   ★

Many of Whitman's finest visionary poems resist interpretation in terms of either of two very common ways of describing the thrust of his work as a whole—that which sees him as
implicitly denying reality to the outside world because he
could, like the spider, spin everything out of himself (needing
no fixed points to attach the web to, apparently); or else
because, reversing the direction of the flow, he could absorb
everything into himself, turning objective into subjective,
the world into a dependent extension of the imperial self.
Even so normally perceptive a critic as Quentin Anderson
has told us that "no such category as *nature* or *mineral* was
allowed to stand in the way of [his] thrust toward assimi-
lation. Nature, we may say, had no separate existence for
Whitman."

True enough, we may be tempted to say, if we stress
"separate" strongly enough. But the nature any of us can
know must always first be perceived, and human perception
necessarily contains an irreducible subjective element. Perception is active, purposive, selective—requiring, with senses
like hearing and sight, an act of attention. But we may, and
often do, turn off our attention, not hear, not see. To perceive
the world is, in some sense, to "assimilate" it, to let it come
in, or to search it out. No doubt Whitman, with his
Emersonian-Romantic heritage, gave special emphasis in his
thinking to the subjective aspect of experience. It is perfectly
easy to find illustrative quotations. "I am large, I contain
multitudes. . . . Copious as you are I absorb you all in myself, and become the master myself," and so on, and on. An
unsympathetic reading can easily be supported by such chill-
ing statements of belief.

The conclusion about Whitman's vision that Anderson
has drawn might seem logically to follow: Whitman, he
writes, was a poet "for whom the pictorial is simply unre-

solved material and is peripheral." Or, in other words, what is "not me" is not really *real*. But if Whitman sometimes entertained such ideas—which are implied by Emerson's early philosophy, and ultimately by any form of subjective Idealism—his greatest visionary poems do not support them. To deduce their meaning not from the poems themselves but from statements of belief that may be found scattered through the poet's other works is to misread them. A sympathetic reader would be justified in finding them anticipating Whitehead in avoiding "the fallacy of misplaced concreteness" and pointing toward a philosophy of organism, actual occasions, concreteness, and process.

"There Was a Child Went Forth," for instance, might be described as a poem about "becoming" what one has experienced but certainly not as denying reality to the objects of experience. *That* thought is explicitly entertained in the poem ("is it all flashes and specks?") and in the end implicitly rejected: if the mature self is real, that which the child "look'd upon" and "became" must be real also. In effect, the strongly felt reality of the other, the experienced, guarantees the reality of the self. If the past should prove unreal, what would make the future immune to skeptical doubt? But the whole poem leads in exactly the opposite direction, toward the confidence expressed in the last line: both the child now become a man and all that became a part of him are real in a sense that time cannot destroy.

To be sure, this visionary extension of the self and the experienced world in time rests upon no logic of belief stated in the poem.[6] The "doubts of night-time" and the threatening

6 But compare Whitehead's discussion of what he calls "eternal objects" in *Process and Reality*, *passim*; and also of the relation of "becoming" to "being" (p. 23), which might be thought of as an abstract statement of the theme of the poem.

thought that what has been so vividly remembered may
"prove unreal" when philosophically considered are simply
rejected, not answered, as the speaker turns to present experience by the water's edge:

> The village on the highland seen from afar at sunset, the
>   river between,
> Shadows, aureola and mist, the light falling on roofs
>   and gables white or brown two miles off,
>
> ....
>
> The horizon's edge, the flying sea-crow, the fragrance
>   of salt marsh and shore mud,
> These became part of that child who went forth every
>   day, and who now goes, and will always go forth
>   every day.

"These" in the last line should be taken to refer both to
the childhood memories and to the present sensuous experiences. Hearing ("the tumbling waves . . . slapping") and
smelling ("fragrance") have joined with seeing to put aside
any further speculation about "the curious whether and how"
of things for an unreasoned, but perfectly "reasonable," trust
in the lasting reality of both the perceived and the perceiver.

The visionary elements in "Song of Myself" are too varied, complex, and important for the effect of the whole poem
to hope that any brief comment could be more than merely
suggestive. Although the description of the poem as an
expression of "inverted mysticism" seems to me to suggest
some inappropriate analogies, it is not wholly wide of the
mark. But to call it a visionary celebration of the person,
every person, seems both to allow better for its variousness
and not to make it a minor relative of a distinguished family.
All the meanings commonly attached to "vision" are impor-

tant in the poem, from the most literal seeing to the most figurative, from "pure" images in which interpretation appears to play no part—though of course images are always at least implicitly symbolic—to explicitly interpreted images, to dream-visions. Statements of belief sometimes precede, sometimes follow, the pure and symbolic images that support the beliefs.

When the central image in the poem, the grass, is first introduced in section 6, the need to interpret it in terms of all that one knows and believes is immediately acknowledged:

> A child said *What is the grass?* fetching it to me with
>   full hands;
> How could I answer the child? I do not know what
>   it is any more than he.

Then come the guesses, attempts to interpret this "uniform hieroglyphic" available to all, guesses that seem both fanciful and random but are held together by the traditional association between the color green and the quality of hope. "The smallest sprout shows there is really no death." What the grass *is* and what it *means* are fused in this section, but when we encounter the image again in the final section, we have shared the experiences that support the hopeful interpretation offered in the final lines of section 6 and so are prepared to see the grass as containing all the meanings it has gathered:

> I bequeath myself to the dirt to grow from the grass I
>   love,
> If you want me again, look for me under your boot-soles.

The poet-priest-prophet speaker at the end has stopped guessing: he knows. But if we are to entertain for ourselves his early guess that the grass is "the handkerchief of the

Lord," with all that this entails, we will have to make our own interpretations—"You will hardly know who I am or what I mean"—encouraged but not specifically instructed by one who has gone before us:

> Failing to fetch me at first keep encouraged,
> Missing me one place search another,
> I stop somewhere waiting for you.

But even this is an oversimplification, since it leaves out of account, among other things, the many sections of the poem that, like section 8 ("The little one sleeps in its cradle"), present what seems to demand, but does not get, interpretation; and leaves out too those quite different sections (section 13 is a fair example) in which the intelligent and purposeful eye interprets what it sees as it sees it, without appearing to block out any of the specifics—"the negro holds firmly the reins of his four horses, the black swags underneath its tied-over chain"—before, at the end, arriving at a meaning that we can share because we have seen how such specific details can be so interpreted:

> I believe in those wing'd purposes,
> And acknowledge red, yellow, white, playing within
>   me,
> And consider green and violet and the tufted crown
>   intentional,
> And do not call the tortoise unworthy because she is not
>   something else,
> And the jay in the woods never studied the gamut, yet
>   trills pretty well to me,
> And the look of the bay mare shames silliness out of me.

Attentive, receptive, literal *seeing* (not "scrutinizing") has led to belief, and such belief in turn leads to a further

stage of imaginative "seeing," as for example in the opening
lines of section 33:

> Space and Time! now I see it is true, what I guessed at,
> What I guess'd when I loaf'd on the grass,
>
> What I guess'd while I lay alone in my bed,
> And again as I walk'd the beach under the paling stars
> of the morning.
>
> My ties and ballasts leave me, my elbows rest in sea-
> gaps,
> I skirt sierras, my palms cover continents,
> I am afoot with my vision.

"Vision" in this passage holds all its possible meanings,
from the visual ("loaf'd on the grass . . . paling stars of the
morning") to the visionary, which no longer needs to be only
"guessed at" because it can in some inner sense be "seen." In
a poem too rich for any approach to exhaust it, this two-way
process, from perception to interpretation and back to fresh
perception, in turn leading to belief-laden vision, seems to
me to be too important an element to go as unremarked as
it has.

What James Miller has called, correctly as it seems to
me, the "imaginative fusion of the poet and the reader" in
"Crossing Brooklyn Ferry"[7] occurs in some sense, I should
suppose, in any successful poem, but here it is at once the
achievement and the subject of the poem, as the opening lines
make clear:

> FLOOD-TIDE below me! I see you face to face!
> Clouds of the west—sun there half an hour high—I see you
> also face to face.

7 J. E. Miller, Jr., *A Critical Guide to Leaves of Grass* (Chicago, 1957), 80–
89.

> Crowds of men and women attired in the usual costumes,
>   how curious you are to me!
> On the ferry-boats the hundreds and hundreds that cross,
>   returning home, are more curious to me than you
>   suppose,
> And you that shall cross from shore to shore years hence are
>   more to me, and more in my meditations, than you
>   might suppose.

To such imaginative seeing, neither time nor place is a barrier. Future generations can be "seen" by the poet because they will see some day what he sees now, and feel as he does. And we can share the poet's vision if we can share his feelings— made available to us in the poem. "Just as you feel when you look on the river, so I felt." Through the power of his words, symbols, style, the poet can at once foresee our experience and let us share his. What makes it possible, poetically, for his words to accomplish this two-way sharing is chiefly the richness and vividness of the visual details like those that make up the bulk of section 3, in which line after line begins with "watched," "saw," or "look'd." Without these very specific visual images, the last section's request to the reader— "Consider, you who peruse me, whether I may not in unknown ways be looking upon you"—would seem weakly fanciful, and the visionary halo seen by the poet over his own and the reader's heads a merely sentimental indulgence:

> Fly on, sea-birds! fly sideways, or wheel in large circles
>   high in the air;
> Receive the summer sky, you water, and faithfully
>   hold it till all downcast eyes have time to take it
>   from you!
> Diverge, fine spokes of light, from the shape of my
>   head, or any one's head, in the sunlit water!

The fact that the Brooklyn ferry has been replaced by the Brooklyn Bridge does not prevent our sharing Whitman's vision of the "fine spokes of light," as Hart Crane would later make clear in another great visionary poem. The "objects" gazed at in the poem with "loving and thirsting eyes"—objects that have proved "dumb, beautiful ministers," creating the "necessary film," the halo to which even the smoke from the foundry chimneys has contributed—are assumed to be "real," whether perceived or not. But they are available, both to the poet and to us, only as "appearances" which, because they are neither wholly transparent nor wholly opaque, must be and can be interpreted.

Properly interpreted, the objects, though "dumb" in themselves, unable to speak to us unambiguously, may be seen as translucent. The very subjectivity of the nonanalytic way of seeing that is consistently reenacted in the poem permits and invites the reader to substitute his own experience for the poet's, as it promotes the poet's realization of the unity of seer and seen. So the poem that has begun with the literally visual "flood-tide" and clouds seen "face to face" has earned its right to the interpretation offered in its final line—"Great or small, you furnish your parts toward the soul."

"Out of the Cradle Endlessly Rocking," which I sometimes think is Whitman's greatest poem, works very differently. If it is to be called a visionary poem, as I think it should be, "vision" must be expanded to a metaphor for "perception" by whatever sense allows us to interpret truly the larger world of which we are a part. Senses at once more primitive and less ambiguous than ordinary seeing because less dependent on verbal symbols and conceptual thinking play the major role here. We do not so much see as hear and feel the images in this beautiful "reminiscence." If what is whispered

to the child by the sea at the end is called a "vision," the word
is equivalent to an outlook, a state of mind—and of emo-
tion—a faith. Whitman seldom wrote just this way, and never
again so successfully.

The image introduced in the opening line and developed
throughout is primarily "kinesthetic," body-feeling, not visual: "Out of the cradle endlessly *rocking.*" As infants we are
comforted by being rocked, are quieted, soothed, made to
feel secure. The last lines return to the whole body as the
source of perception, though now the kinesthetic report is
supported by olfactory and auditory images:

> (Or like some old crone rocking the cradle, swathed in
>   sweet garments, bending aside,)
> The sea whisper'd to me.

Though we may form a generalized and very personal
image of an "old crone," what chiefly moves us here is the
rocking, the pleasant *smell* (like the smell of the mother in
"There Was a Child Went Forth"), and the *sound* of the
"strong and delicious" (taste?) word being whispered by the
sea, the word "death," which is surely not "delicious" either
to child or adult except as this poem makes it seem so. These
images do not bring us "appearances" requiring interpretation as "Crossing Brooklyn Ferry" does: they seem to speak
for themselves of realities that cannot be doubted. Without
undue distortion, the effect of the poem could almost be said
to be visceral—or better yet, because *visceral* may suggest the
purely physical, without any mental component, *unitary.* At
any rate, it is about as "unphilosophic," as little abstractly
"conceptual," as a poem, a verbal artifact, could be.

But of course words get their meanings not just from
the personal memories they call up but from associations de-

veloped in long social usage. In this sense, too, the poem depends less on the visual rendered visionary than was Whitman's practice in earlier poems, for both "sea" and "mother" have universal or archetypal associations that invite a Jungian reading. Sea and mother are equated in the poem, explicitly in the end, and both are ambivalent, the source of life and death, at once sweet-smelling rocker of the cradle and "savage old mother," "old crone." But though the poem may invite such an archetypal reading, it does not demand it, for the images rest on too concretely personal, including visual, experiences to need theoretic explication. The poem is at once conceptually mysterious and imaginatively clear as a reminiscence of a little boy's discovery and final acceptance of love and death.

"When Lilacs Last in the Dooryard Bloom'd" is both Whitman's last truly great long poem and a visionary poem in whatever positive sense we may use the word, from what is seen and found meaningful to what is first imagined and then found to be true to what is revealed in the song of the bird, in a "vision" reminiscent of the way "the word of the Lord came unto Abram in a vision." Its chief images, like those in "Out of the Cradle," are heavily freighted with associations that have a long history, but unlike the earlier poem it moves toward the resolution of its final lines through a pattern of visual, auditory, and olfactory images the implications of which are clear enough to suggest that the structure of the poem was carefully thought out. This, and the explicitness of its references to the several kinds of vision woven into its movement, make it seem Whitman's most consciously artful visionary poem. When the dark cloud that had hidden the star in the beginning has been dissipated in the end, the initial dependence on literal visual perception has been transcended and fully participatory perception attained, in lines whose sound and sense blend to support the visionary implications of a pattern of images and rhythms that involve the whole sensuous self:

> Lilac and star and bird twined in the chant of my soul,
> There in the fragrant pines and the cedars dusk and
>   dim.

★   ★   ★

Like the great visionary poems written in the fifties, a good many of the shorter poems of the sixties, especially those included in "Drum-Taps," exhibit Whitman's characteristic search for the unseen meanings of the seen. Because of their brevity and consequent compression of movement, these poems are handier examples of Whitman's visionary practice than the more complex long ones, but for the same reasons they are more open to misinterpretation. To read them either as anticipating the assumption behind later Imagist poems that what is seen speaks for itself, needing no subjective interpretation, or as implying the relative unimportance of perceptible "fact" in comparison with intuited or reasoned "meaning," is to misunderstand them.

"A Noiseless Patient Spider," for instance, has been commonly read as Whitman's confession that his own "web"—his book and his life—was as much spun out of himself alone, out of wish and need, as the spider's was spun out of its own body. That Whitman did consciously strive to realize an ideal self-image in his life and his book is clear enough, but the poem can be read in this purely subjective way only by taking the phrase "out of itself" as the sufficient key to the whole poem, disregarding the fact that the spider first had to have some support to launch forth from and then had to trust the air currents to bring it to something solid, again external to itself, to attach its web to. In effect, such a solipsistic reading would either do away with the external world of fact or see it as wholly plastic to our needs. Either way, there would be no way of distinguishing between real webs and imagined ones.

But Whitman was not such a poor observer of how things go in the world, with spiders or with people. The analogy he sees between the spider and himself rests on more than is suggested by the single phrase "out of itself" describing one aspect of the spinning of the web. The "little promontory" that the spider must have to launch forth from is comparable to the poet's background, the external facts that have shaped him, like those recited in "There Was a Child Went Forth." If the spider's effort to spin a web, once it trusts itself to the air currents, is to succeed, it must, as the poem says, "catch somewhere" on something solid, outside itself, capable of anchoring the other end of the filament. Only then, after the initial filament has been anchored at both ends, can the spinning of the intricately structured web be begun. Neither the spider nor the poet can be assured in advance of the success of the venture. Unpredictable air currents for the one and experiences yet to be lived for the other make both efforts acts of faith—faith in the world as well as in the self.

A similarly subjective misreading is often given "When I Heard the Learn'd Astronomer." Whitman's leaving the lecture hall to go out where he could simply look up at the stars can imply momentary boredom with dry facts and figures without implying Whitman's lack of interest in, or knowledge of, the physical, "objective" cosmos being revealed by the new science of astronomy. In fact, we know from sources outside the poem that he followed the latest developments in astronomy—resulting, interestingly enough, chiefly from improved telescopes, technological extensions of our literal vision—with keen interest. "Song of Myself" and other poems are sprinkled with words and passages that sometimes come directly from lectures heard and books read that altered nineteenth-century man's vision of his place in the ever larger, and, as Whitman saw it, ever more mysterious, perceptible universe. When the poet walked out and "look'd up in perfect silence at the stars," he was not repudiating objective knowledge in favor of pure subjectivity but was acting out his need to experience for himself the personal dimensions of knowledge. The way he saw the stars owed a good deal to the observations of astronomers using the new, more powerful telescopes. If we feel we must give the poem a larger meaning than this that will be consistent with the rest of Whitman's poetry, it could be that abstract knowledge is unimportant until it is personally experienced as vision. Knowing how far the light rays reaching him from the unimaginably distant stars had traveled certainly had something to do with his perception of the moist night air as "mystical."

Another often-reprinted poem implying the continued importance of visual images for Whitman, "Cavalry Crossing a Ford," is open to two opposite misinterpretations. It can be read as though the picture the poem creates for us in words were in effect an abstract design found in nature, a "fact" without any "meaning." Read this way, it is a descriptive poem of the sort that Imagists would later say they intended to write. But since it would be surprising to find Whitman writing about something that held no personal significance for himself in his role as the "sayer of words" who would teach us how to see, we may be tempted to go to the opposite extreme in interpretation and "behold" in the "picture" the poem draws for us of the long line of cavalrymen crossing the stream the shape of a cross surrounded by green islands of hope.

But such a reading in Christian terms, though to be sure not contradicted by anything in the poem, seems to me as unsatisfactory as the proto-Imagist reading. (It might seem satisfactory if this were the only poem of Whitman's we knew, or if we did not know it was Whitman's.) Whitman had attended St. Ann's Sunday School in Brooklyn, and he had a personal feeling for the distant cavalrymen: they were not mere external "objects of perception" to him. In the future, for many of them, he knew lay the suffering and death encountered in "A Sight in Camp," in which the dead soldiers seemed to have reenacted Christ's death. The cross would suggest to him the death of the innocent, as the color green would suggest hope. Such associations were a part of his cultural heritage, available to him to express his feelings about the war and the young men who fought and died in it. The poem may be read as implicitly religious in feeling without being explicitly Christian—though Whitman himself would very likely not have made such a distinction.

"A Sight in Camp" is surely one of Whitman's most moving short poems, but any attempt to clarify the unorthodox Christology of the last lines could only result in a diminishment of the poem:

> I think this face is the face of the Christ himself,
> Dead and divine and brother of all, and here again he lies.

Since "dead" and "divine" and "brother" (avatar?) all receive equal emphasis, any attempt to locate the poem within a recognized creedal position must ignore some of the evidence. The poem has consisted of detailed, precise visual images until, at the end, it moves, with "I think," from the visual to the visionary, from implicitly interpretive perception to explicit conscious interpretation. What does all this mean? Who is this unknown dead soldier really? At this point where seeing stops and thinking begins, contradictions also begin. I think we may doubt that Whitman consciously intended the poem to be either ecumenical in spirit or offensive to any sectarian readers. The way he *saw* the three dead soldiers simply led him to think of them as he did. Visionary experience does not by itself dictate an unambiguous rational interpretation. "Young man I think I know you—I think. . . ."

★   ★   ★

Whitman's poetry began to diminish in imaginative power when the "seen," the perceived world, no longer seemed to lead directly into the "unseen," to visions of the completion of what was potential in the seen. Reasons for the decline of the late poetry may of course be found in biography—the aging process, Whitman's failing health, the weakening of imaginative vigor (whatever that may mean)—but whatever the causes, the results, viewed from within the poems themselves, may be seen as a departure from Whitman's earlier visionary practice. In the end, he wrote meditative, not visionary poems.

How that development affected his last attempt at a long visionary poem is clear enough in "Passage to India," first published in 1868. The poem has struck most modern readers as deeply flawed, and not only, I believe, because today most of us have lost both faith in America as a new, unfallen Garden of Eden and hope that technology will bring the millenium. What weakens it as a poem, apart from the way history seems to have betrayed Whitman, is chiefly the vagueness of its celebration of the "myths and fables of eld," in contrast with the specific clarity of the imagery drawn from the present. Since the poem asks us to see such "strong light works of engineers" as the Suez Canal, the transcontinental railroad, and the Atlantic cable as the fulfillment of the "dreams . . . bibles and legends" of the past, the disparity between past and present, as they are realized in the poem, is fatal to the achievement of Whitman's explicit intention.

Uneven in the imaginative power of the sections devoted alternately, after the two introductory sections, to past and present, with what is imaginatively "seen" in the present (in section 3, for example) leading to a hope never fulfilled within the poem—that "Nature and Man shall be disjoined and diffused no more"—the poem fails to move from sight to vision until the soul's "leap of faith" in the prayer of section 8, and then concludes, in the final section, with the hope of a future "passage to more than India," on seas totally uncharted, voyages trusted not because literal vision has enabled the poet to envision them but because they are on seas simply known to be "the seas of God." In effect, the poem's hope for the future rests not on learning to see as the Psalmist did when he was led to declare that "the heavens reveal the glory of God" but on a religious faith that seems inadequately prepared for.

Of course it may well be that hope for the future in our time can be nourished only in the life of prayer, and the prayer in this poem seems to me to be a beautiful and moving one, perhaps the greatest prayer in American poetry, but poetry and religion are not identical, except perhaps in what is called "devotional poetry"; and if we were to think of "Passage to India" as essentially a devotional poem, it would still be weakened either by the vagueness in image and diction of its presentation of the past, in which the meaning of "the elder religions" and "deep diving bibles and legends" is never

really clarified, or, alternatively, by the way the opening
promise to "Eclaircise the myths Asiatic, the primitive
fables" seems intended to be fulfilled in section 6 by the recognition of Columbus as the greatest visionary of all. Surely
the ultimate hidden meaning of the Eastern religions the
poem refers to is no better disclosed by the discoverer of
America than by Western technology, exemplified in "the
strong light works" of American engineers.

If "Passage to India" must be called a failed visionary
poem, "The Base of All Metaphysics," dating from 1871,
may be described as a meditation on the superiority of love
to any visionary interpretation of experience, here called
"metaphysics," despite the fact that neither Socrates nor
Christ would appear to have presented us with any "metaphysical" system. The divorce of belief from experience suggested by this use of "metaphysics" is apparent in the poem
also in the purely metaphoric use of "see" in the final lines:

AND now gentlemen,
A word I give to remain in your memories and minds,
As base and finale too for all metaphysics.

(So to the students the old professor,
At the close of his crowded course.)

Having studied the new and antique, the Greek and Germanic
    systems,
Kant having studied and stated, Fichte and Schelling and Hegel,
Stated the lore of Plato, and Socrates greater than Plato,
And greater than Socrates sought and stated, Christ divine
    having studied long,
I see reminiscent to-day those Greek and Germanic systems,
See the philosophies all, Christian churches and tenets see,
Yet underneath Socrates clearly see, and underneath Christ
    the divine I see,

The dear love of man for his comrade, the attraction of friend
    to friend,
Of the well-married husband and wife, of children and parents,
Of city for city and land for land.

I find wisdom in this poem, and psychic health, but little else to suggest that the poet who wrote it is the poet of "There Was a Child Went Forth" or "Crossing Brooklyn Ferry." The poem seems to say that the differences between ways of seeing-interpreting the world of our experience are finally unimportant.

The impression that "The Base of All Metaphysics" provides a true indication of the direction in which Whitman was moving is only partially dispelled by his last major attempt at a visionary poem, "The Mystic Trumpeter," dating from 1872, in which "visionary" means "prophetic," in much the same sense that the Book of Revelation was intended to be prophetic: an apocalyptic dream-vision of a "reborn race" inhabiting "a perfect world" after the end of time as we have known it, when, perhaps recalling John's "no more tears," the poet foresees "war, sorrow, suffering gone—the rank earth purged—nothing but joy left!"

Not surprisingly, the poet's vision of a new heaven and a new earth rests upon his ability to interpret notes sounded with "a vigor more than earth's" by a trumpeter described as "unseen" and "bodiless." Whitman is closer now to Blake hearing "the Holy Word, / That walked among the ancient trees" than he had been in his greater early visionary poems. The joyful vision of the future offered in the last section, to "renew . . . a languishing faith and hope," seems not to grow out of the presentations of feudal pageantry, love's solvent, war's "terrible tableaus," or "the wrongs of ages" that have preceded it without in any way preparing us for it. The darkness of "utter defeat" has been dispelled by light from an unseen source.

The "terrible doubt of appearances" that had come to the poet early, only to be dispelled by the touch of a comrade's hand or the smell of salt marshes, has returned to trouble the ill and aging poet, as he tells us in a poem dating from the year before his death, "Apparitions":

> A VAGUE mist hanging 'round half the pages:
> (Sometimes how strange and clear to the soul,
> That all these solid things are indeed but apparitions,
> concepts, non-realities.)

In a less despondent mood he could still find the "nonrealities" "grand" in themselves, but "puzzling," containing, it would seem, no hints of the "unseen" with which, in the poem, they stand in sharp contrast. In "Grand Is the Seen," both seen and unseen are to be respected, but the light of comprehension that endows the seen with grandeur appears to be the gift of a faith unrelated to any sort of perception:

> GRAND is the seen, the light, to me—grand are the sky and
> stars,
> Grand is the earth, and grand are lasting time and space,
> And grand their laws, so multiform, puzzling, evolutionary;
> But grander far the unseen soul of me, comprehending,
> endowing all those,
> Lighting the light, the sky and stars, delving the earth, sailing
> the sea,
> (What were all those, indeed, without thee, unseen soul? of
> what amount without thee?)
> More evolutionary, vast, puzzling, O my soul!
> More multiform far—more lasting thou than they.

Experience now, which had once provided Whitman with occasions that seemed to offer grounds for their own interpretation, no longer seems endowed with intrinsic meaning.

In effect, the life lived and "the life to come" have split apart. True vision now seems hardly less apocalyptic than that prophesied by Isaiah in 60:19: "The sun shall be no more thy light by day; neither for brightness shall the moon give light unto thee: but the Lord shall be unto thee an everlasting light, and thy God thy glory." Whitman's intuitive, pared-down, Quakerish faith in God, freedom, and immortality was left, but ordinary experience had ceased to be translucent and so provided no basis for the kind of visionary poetry he had once written. Earlier, many of his visionary poems might be glossed by quotations from *Process and Reality*: to perceive is to participate in occasions the very nature of which moves us beyond the realism/idealism and the science/religion choices toward an organismic philosophy of becoming. The visionary poets who followed in his wake would have to start once again where he had started, finding enough meaning in personal experience to seem to justify an unprovable faith in the coherence of the seen and unseen.

As if to strengthen such faith in later readers and later poets, the dying poet decided to place "Unseen Buds" directly after "Grand Is the Seen." In its less-guarded and understated way, it foreshadows Williams' later "Spring and All" ("By the road to the contagious hospital"):

UNSEEN buds, infinite, hidden well,
Under the snow and ice, under the darkness, in every square
    or cubic inch,
Germinal, exquisite, in delicate lace, microscopic, unborn,
Like babes in wombs, latent, folded, compact, sleeping;
Billions of billions, and trillions of trillions of them waiting,
(On earth and in the sea—the universe—the stars there in the
    heavens,)
Urging slowly, surely forward, forming endless,
And waiting ever more, forever more behind.

CHAPTER III

Hart Crane

"Only in Darkness Is Thy Shadow Clear"

At the very center of *The Bridge*, as the "Cape Hatteras" section moves to its triumphal conclusion, Crane declares the purpose of the whole poem, and of his poetic career, as he saw them then: to reexpress in contemporary terms, and thus make available for a later time, the vision of Whitman, the "joyous seer." In "Cape Hatteras," at any rate, he had largely succeeded, and he knew it and said so. With the airplane to symbolize a further conquest of space beyond that suggested to Whitman by the Suez Canal, the transcontinental railroad, and the Atlantic cable, Crane had extended Whitman's "span of consciousness" beyond "the Open Road," beyond even the solid earth itself: "My hand / in yours, / Walt Whitman— / so—," "thy vision is reclaimed!"[1]

This could seem no empty boast at the end of "Cape Hatteras," but what about the poem as a whole? American history from the perspective of the twenties, the scientific orthodoxy of the time, and Crane's own personal experience were all far less easy to see in Whitmanic terms than the pioneering conquest of space achieved by the Wright brothers at Kitty Hawk. All along, Crane's confidence in his major work had been painfully intermittent and his illuminations fitful and unpredictable, even with the ever-more-frequent aid of alcohol. When he came to write his introductory "Proem"—the invocation "To Brooklyn Bridge"—after several troubled years of alternating hope and despair and many efforts to explain to friends and patron why the major work had been so long delayed, he could express only the hope that the meaning he had seen in the bridge had found, or some time would find, expression in a form adequate to the vision, a form that would truly "lend a myth to God." Meanwhile,

1 *The Collected Poems of Hart Crane*, ed. Waldo Frank (Black and Gold Edition; New York, 1946), 39. All quotations from Crane's poems are taken from this edition.

the "Proem" in effect says, he would have to be content with the knowledge that the vision would desert him again as it had so often in the past, taking on the quality of an "apparition" when he descended into the subway to go home to Brooklyn.

But might it be possible to turn to advantage his subway and theater experiences, and even the recalcitrant intellectual climate of the age, using them to test the validity of his epiphanies? If the bridge's shadow could be seen in the darkness, might that not be construed as evidence that his affirmation of its meaning was not sentimental or weakly "idealistic"? Of course, if the darkness became total, as seemed quite possible, there would be no shadow. So the "pariah" and "bedlamite," as the accepted poetic and social standards of the age must make him seem, could only go on waiting under the piers and hoping for further assurance that he had moved beyond the "threshold of the prophet's pledge" in the direction of that "heaven of the Jews" that he could neither believe in nor stop being haunted by. He had experienced moments of illumination—even once in a dentist's chair, as he wrote to a friend—when he believed that he had really "seen night lifted," but now he could only wait some more and try to hope that his attempt to make Whitman's vision available again, in an antivisionary style for an antivisionary age, would eventually seem a successful "stab at truth."

★   ★   ★

Such a reading of "To Brooklyn Bridge"—as expressing hope deferred and implying Crane's half-suppressed realization that he had failed to do what he had set out to do—is borne out by later passages in *The Bridge*, by the structure of the whole, and by the pervasively oxymoronic style. He had studied what there was to be seen, he tells us in "The Tunnel," studied the lights, refractions, faces, searched them all, but in the end he could still only hope that someday he would

> learn each famous sight
> And watch the curtain lift in hell's despite;
> You'll find the garden in the third act dead,
> Finger your knees—and wish yourself in bed
> With tabloid crime-sheets perched in easy sight.

In the subway where he meets the ghost of Poe, whose sensibility and outlook were so much more like his own than Whitman's was, he finds that

> The phonographs of hades in the brain
> Are tunnels that rewind themselves, and love
> A burnt match skating in a urinal.

But still he could not do without the hope that someday, somehow, he would achieve, or be granted, something like the vision that Whitman seemed best to have expressed. The "muffled slaughter" of dawn's light could not be the whole story:

> O cruelly to inoculate the brinking dawn
> With antennae toward worlds that glow and sink;—
> To spoon us out more liquid than the dim
> Locution of the eldest star, and pack
> The conscience navelled in the plunging wind,
> Umbilical to call—and straightway die!

For beyond words there was the memory of the Word:

> O caught like pennies beneath soot and steam,
> Kiss of our agony thou gatherest;
> Condensed, thou takest all—shrill ganglia
> Impassioned with some song we fail to keep.
> And yet, like Lazarus, to feel the slope,
> The sod and billow breaking,—lifting ground,

　　　—A sound of waters bending astride the sky
　　　Unceasing with some Word that will not die.

For a poet to turn from words and the perceptible world
they call up to the Word of Scripture is in effect to admit
poetic failure; for a visionary poet in the company Crane
hoped to join, personal failure too. Still, he could not give up
the hope that with the help of Whitman's words and the Revealed Word of Scripture—or of Poetry, the poet's "scripture"?—he might yet write the song of praise that would be
at once his own Te Deum and "Psalm of Cathay," "Deity's
glittering Pledge." But when he turns back to the real bridge
in the opening lines of "Atlantis," he finds it speaking to him
only an *as if* word: "As though a god were issue of the
strings." So, with Whitman's example in "Passage to India"
before him, he ends "Atlantis" and the whole poem with a
prayer, or rather prayers, not to the "nameless" Transcendent
that Whitman had addressed but first to the disciplined poetic
imagination itself—"O Thou steeled Cognizance"—then to
"Love" and to "Atlantis," the lost continent. Led by the poet's
"steeled Cognizance" beyond "time's realm" of "Sight, sound,
and flesh" over a "Bridge of Fire" with the anemone, or flower
of Easter and the Resurrection, and the "tolling star" of
Christmas that "bleeds infinity" to help guide him, the speaker
appears to be moving toward his goal. But "Is it Cathay. . . ?" For answer, he can hear only "whispers" from far
away.

★　★　★

With the poem itself suggesting the desperateness of the leap
necessary for the movement from sensation to meaning,
should we call *The Bridge* a "visionary poem" in the sense I
have let Whitman establish? Crane himself of course insists,

both within the poem and in prose statements of his purpose, that we should, and what was intended as the controlling image, the bridge, makes us expect it to be. It starts off as one in "To Brooklyn Bridge," and "Cape Hatteras," which makes the poet's purpose explicit, fits our expectations for a visionary poem. Finally, there are many passages and several sections or subsections that at least begin as we should expect, "Harbor Dawn" especially.

But most of what Crane "saw"—perceived with the senses, experienced—did not satisfy his need for meaning or wholeness, or further his intention for his poem. So he fell back on mythic history—Columbus and Pocahontas and "the spirit of the land"—and on the storehouse of traditional religious allusions. But myth that is known to be myth— "mere myth"—is not psychically supportive. Nor are the explicit Christian allusions, which are given so little content that they seem the product of nostalgia rather than of any sort of belief. And so, as we read through the poem, the meaning of "visionary" as Crane would have us apply it to his poem becomes more and more obscure. Does it have anything, really, to do with what can be literally seen, heard, felt, or sensed? Does it mean "prophetic"? "Imagined"? "Wished"? At any rate, it seems not to mean, finally, either attentively perceived or really known.

The difficulty we experience in locating the poem in Whitmanic visionary terms can be clarified somewhat by noting its relation to three poems by Whitman that Crane alludes to in "Cape Hatteras." In "Out of the Cradle" ("you walked the beach"), Whitman had expressed his sense of being reconciled to the child's discovery of death by becoming one with the experienced natural world of land, sea, and bird; but Crane was trying to relate to something much less concrete, to the "new universe" and "new verities" of science

that Crane, like most other poets of his age, found frightening. In "Passage to India" ("Great Navigator"), we need not
share Whitman's faith in the beneficial effect of technology
for it to seem not wholly implausible, but in "The Bridge,"
except in "Cape Hatteras," technology is usually either absent
or experienced as negative in its effect, like elevators and sub-
ways. In "Song of the Open Road," Whitman could seem
really to believe that the seen led on into the unseen, so that
the road would be open all the way, even beyond ever-new
horizons; but for Crane, time—the enemy—brought the
road to a dead end, if not in "Cape Hatteras," then in the
other sections of the poem—"Quaker Hill," for example,
where there are "cows that see no other thing / Than grass
and snow," but the poet, gazing from the same vantage point,
says he has "seen death's stare in slow survey / From four
horizons that no one relates." "Cape Hatteras" remains a
wonderful *tour de force*, but a comment in one of Crane's
letters is revealing: "If only America were half as worthy
today to be spoken of as Whitman spoke of it fifty years ago
there might be something for me to say."[2]

The structure of the poem also fails to support the purpose Crane had declared in "Cape Hatteras." There have been
too many discussions of how the poem fails structurally despite its brilliant passages to warrant more than a few remarks
here. The uneven quality of the sections and subsections has
generally been admitted even by ardent admirers of the work
as a whole, but not so often noted is the way the elaborate
structural arrangement seems to owe more to *The Waste Land*
than to any poem by Whitman. The analytic arrangement
and titling, the epigraphs (in languages Crane could not read),
the marginal notes—all give an impression of learning that

2   *The Letters of Hart Crane*, ed. Brom Weber (Berkeley, 1965), 261.

the poem fails to support. One of Crane's announced purposes was to "answer" *The Waste Land*, and he appears to be trying to do it in Eliot's own terms. Strengthening our impression that Eliot's poem was his model is Crane's insistence in a letter to a reviewer who had found the poem lacking "integrated unity and development" that "*The Bridge* is at least as complicated in its structure and inferences as *The Wasteland*—perhaps more so," and so would yield its meaning after many readings and much study.[3] It had taken him, he said, nearly five years to understand Eliot's poem well enough to see the unity. The poem is weakest when the plan calls for dramatic verse, strongest in its lyric sections, as in parts of "Van Winkle," but the pretentiousness of the effort to seem learned affects our response to the whole poem, even to the most authentic and moving expressions of hope. In "Cape Hatteras," for example, where the effort to reclaim Whitman's vision seems most successful, the use of "Panis Angelicus" to describe Whitman as a modern Pan, god of the woods, fields, and flocks, when the Latin phrase refers to the *bread* of the Holy Communion, seriously weakens the climax of a moving poem. Is the poet, we begin to wonder, trying to "lie to us"—and to himself—in an effort to charm us back into the "tribal morn" when the innocent eye could find the "visionary" real? The stylistic brilliance of much of the poem might almost do that, momentarily, if we were not confronted with so many examples of pretentiousness. The poem will last because of the beauty of many of its parts, but it could hardly fail more completely to "reclaim" Whitman's vision. Nor does it in any way really answer *The Waste Land*. In it, the promise of transcendence seems to have disappeared from contemporary society with the Wright brothers.

3   *Ibid.*, 350.

The style, too, undermines Crane's purpose. Irony and paradox were demanded in Modernist verse, along with various types of ambiguity, but paradox as it has been used in the long tradition of paradoxy in poetry, philosophy, and theology can have the effect of refining meaning, ridding it of impurities, testing affirmations against what makes them difficult. Oxymoron, though, denies meaning: the two contraries brought together just cancel each other out, leaving nothing at all as a remainder that can be said. Oxymoron seems a poetic tic again and again in *The Bridge*. In a poem in which "cupolas" are seen as "abysmal" and "light" is only "unshadow," so that we cannot distinguish up from down or light from dark (for in total darkness there can be no shadow), we cannot expect to discover any meaningful affirmation of an "intrinsic Myth" such as Crane thought Whitman's was. Ambiguity, irony, paradox, and oxymoron were Crane's verbal defenses against charges of naïveté and idealism, his bow to "the modern temper" and the expectations of the most sophisticated readers of poetry. But the price he paid for the safety thus gained was that, though *The Bridge* seems to demand to be called a visionary poem, the darkness in it seems more real than the light.

★ ★ ★

Near the end of his short life, Crane gained considerable insight into the difficulties he had faced as he tried to reclaim Whitman's vision in terms drawn from and relevant to the twenties. "The Broken Tower," written after the publication of *The Bridge*—in which he now believed he had attempted the impossible—tells us, implicitly, more about his aims and the obstacles to their accomplishment than his defensive letters and essays. Although it is full of apparently concrete images drawn from the perceptible world, from the "bell-rope," "knell," and "cathedral lawn" of the first stanza to the

"slip," "circles," and "lake" of the final stanzas, Crane seems
not so much "seeing" as manipulating images, prompted by
the multiple connotations of the words, at one or two re-
moves from the things and actions the words denote.

The bell that awakens the monks for the earliest religious
service of the day knells mournfully for him, as for a funeral,
announcing not a new day but a spent day. Nostalgic about
the historic faith he feels cut off from, he cannot join in the
sung service of praise but can only "wander the cathedral
lawn / From pit to crucifix, feet chill on steps from hell."
The bells themselves, the sounds of their ringing, and even
the stars and the sun have become painful reminders of a dead
faith. The "heavens" seem painfully ambiguous in what they
declare, and ancient rumors are scarcely to be trusted. Hearing only "prostrate" echoes from the broken tower, he must
build a new structure in response to the "visible wings of
silence sown / In azure circles" if he is to fulfill the destiny
for which he still feels he "entered the broken world"—that
is, to "trace the visionary company of love."

But whether his words, with their "broken intervals,"
are "cognate" with the Word scored long ago by the rumored
"tribunal monarch" to whom the monks had sung their
praise, or even whether his version of the Word is capable of
nourishing hope or instead is "cleft to despair," is no longer
clear to him. The "angelus" he has really heard, not just read
about, has both prompted him to prayer and intensified those
"internal wars" that have left him no answer to his questions.
But have his questions been the right ones? "Could blood
hold such a lofty tower / As flings the question true?"

The new bell tower will be built of words by the power
of poetic imagination, not of stone ("Not stone can jacket
heaven"), and it will not so much soar upward toward the

heavens as project, as a "slip" or pier does, into that "quiet lake" that is Crane's reduced version of the "sea of faith" whose ebbing Matthew Arnold had mourned. We must look down, not up, to see such a slip. It symbolizes the "intrinsic Myth" of earth, not heaven, and is personally experienced, not rumored. It is the earth itself that now "lifts love in its shower." But if towers and piers, sea and lake, stone building blocks and "pebbles" are all equivalent and interchangeable, and we must "lift down" our eyes to see them, the perceptible things of the real earth are not what has moved the poem but words and ideas. Or, in the terms suggested by Blake's motto, any "seeing" there is in the poem has been done "with," not "through," the eye.

The internal war alluded to ("The angelus of wars my chest evokes") and the vast gap between Crane's experience and his aspirations, conveyed in the ironic style of the early Eliot, have produced a poem in which aspiration is simultaneously expressed and denied, achievement at once claimed and belittled. Heaven is either the imaginative construct of a lost religious faith or a projection of the unconscious, and love either the ultimate content of the Christian Revelation or a sexual erection (*swelling* a tower), as we may choose. As an example of what Crane could do with "the logic of metaphor," the poem is brilliant; but it does not say anything positive without simultaneously taking it back, and the "logic" of the poem's metaphors seems governed more by thought than by any kind of sensuous experience.

But what it does not "say" it reveals: Crane's growing insight into his problem as a would-be visionary poet. If love were really to come as a refreshing shower from an unsealed earth rather than from the rejected "commodious" sky, the things of earth would have to be attended to, seen, felt, fully

perceived in all their suchness, and found to be spiritually
nourishing, not just glanced at and used as springboards for
imaginative flights. But Crane's own experience—of love,
for instance—had revealed only a broken world and a burnt
match in a urinal, and prompted only a warfare of the chest,
so that "echoes" of a lost faith that had once produced "oval
encyclicals" were all he really had. A would-be follower of
Whitman could hardly face greater difficulty. Visionary transcendence in Whitman's greatest poems had not required any
turning away from the perceptible world but a closer, more
imaginative look and a more insightful interpretation.

★   ★   ★

Many of the early poems collected in *White Buildings* may be
read as preparing us for the self-doubts expressed in "The
Broken Tower." "Legend," which opens the collection, ex-
presses the desire to find "some constant harmony" in a
world in which "realities plunge in silence by." Aesop, in
"Black Tambourine," the poem that follows, could find
heaven in comon objects like the tortoise and the hare, but
the modern artist cannot make fables of the roach on the floor
or the "carcass quick with flies"—*his* "realities"—and so
must, Stevens-fashion, turn to art. "Memories of spiritual
gates" are all the modern artist has left, and it may be questioned whether even these are really recalled or just "built,"
as "Emblems of Conduct" and "My Grandmother's Love
Letters" suggest. And "Praise for an Urn" ends with the
speaker's realization that the "inheritances" cannot now be
personally experienced, so that any effort to celebrate the
light will be of doubtful success:

> Still, having in mind gold hair,
> I cannot see that broken brow

And miss the dry sound of bees
Stretching across a lucid space.

Scatter these well-meant idioms
Into the smoky spring that fills
The suburbs, where they will be lost.
They are no trophies of the sun.

Only abstractly, in unfettered imagination, can the unity
with nature that is the subject of "Garden Abstract" be
dreamed: the real apple must be replaced by the "mimic" one
that involves "no memory, nor fear, nor hope." Emerson had
once believed that "in the mud and scum of things / There
alway, alway, something sings," but for Crane, as for Poe,
real apples are not enough, for illuminations come only in
dream, as

Vestiges of the sun that somehow
Filter in to us before we waken.
—"Stark Major"

In such a "crematory lobby" of a world, time is as empty of
meaning as space, so that our world resembles "North Labrador," that "land of leaning ice" where "there is only the shift-
ing of moments / That journey toward no spring." As
Whitehead would soon write and as Stevens implied in "The
Snow Man," a "dead nature" gives no answers.

The "repose" conferred by the sound of willows in "Repose of Rivers"—one of the most moving poems in the collection—is achieved by the music of "pure poetry," in which
the conventions of ordinary language are replaced by the
"logic of metaphor," which exploits the accumulated historical associations of words, mining them for ambiguities. Willows, like cypresses, were once engraved on tombstones as

death symbols, but the sound they make in a gentle wind might also suggest a "sarabande," a slow, stately dance of the living. But such a dance can now only be imagined, not seen, in the city of "scalding unguents." Again, imagination and desire permit the speaker to replace the beaver pond he imagines once having "entered . . . and quickly fled" with an image of the sea "beyond the dykes," where he can hear "wind flaking sapphire." The fact that real beaver ponds resemble the sea only as any body of water resembles any other presents no barrier to the unfettered imagination. Words are what the writer of a pure poem works with, not objects. The repose that is felt at the end of the poem in the line, "And willows could not hold more steady sound," seems fully earned poetically only if we read the poem as we would look at a nonrepresentational painting.

Out of context, "steady" is of course a neutral word: pain can be as steady as pleasure, and is perhaps more likely to be, but we have been prepared here to read it positively, as suggesting release from the earlier "noon's / Tyranny" and "sulfur dreams." More typically, the poems in *White Buildings* make any such movement toward release and fulfillment impossible by creating a stasis in which despair and hope are inseparable, as pain and relief are in "scalding unguents." In "Paraphrase," for instance, morning will bring only a "desperate" light that will bruise the roses and offer "purposeless repose." Moonlight in "Lachrymae Christi" dissolves the world of the senses with "benzine rinsings," revealing the "perfidies of spring" to eyes that have been rendered sightless ("galvanized") by "perjuries": neither what can be seen nor what has been heard or read can be trusted. As though Crane were remembering Rimbaud, as he would later often claim to be in his letters, he writes in "Wine Menagerie" that only disordered senses offer the possibility of vision:

> Invariably when wine redeems the sight,
> Narrowing the mustard scansions of the eyes,
> A leopard ranging always in the brow
> Asserts a vision in the slumbering gaze.

"For the Marriage of Faustus and Helen" strikes me now as chiefly a period piece, in which the oxymoronic irony seems a stylistic tic and only the last stanza of the final section remains really memorable, as Crane drops his guard and declares his trust in imagination:

> Distinctly praise the years, whose volatile
> Blamed bleeding hands extend and thresh the height
> The imagination spans beyond despair,
> Outpacing bargain, vocable and prayer.

The contrast between "At Melville's Tomb," a meditative poem despite the apparent emphasis on seeing in the first stanza, and the first poem of the "Voyages" is instructive. In the lovely tribute to Melville, the "saw" and "watched" of the opening lines are purely figurative and the poem can end on a note of calm acceptance and even celebration. But in "Voyages I," the speaker seems really to be looking at and hearing children playing on the beach, then reflecting on the relation between the seen and the known, before he issues his final warning to the innocents: "The bottom of the sea is cruel." Crane aspired to be a visionary poet, but what he really saw usually awakened only distrust. Nature may look innocent, but looks can be deceptive.

"And yet this great wink of eternity," the sea, can now and then be experienced as numinous and so can prompt the petition expressed in the final stanza of "Voyages II," that we may be open to the epiphanies granted in time:

> Bind us in time, O Seasons clear, and awe.
> O minstrel galleons of Carib fire,

Bequeath us to no earthly shore until
Is answered in the vortex of our grave
The seal's wide spindrift gaze toward paradise.

The sea here is the "mysterium tremendum"—the awful
mystery capable of making one tremble—yet still desirable,
bringing, as the poem puts it in words that come close to
echoing Otto's *The Idea of the Holy*, "sleep, death, desire."
Although Crane is "seeing" primarily with "the mind's eye,"
with the imagination firmly in control at all times, yet the
sea, the islands, and the sunset *have* been seen and are neither
forgotten nor distorted. Not again until "Voyages VI" would
Crane write so beautiful a visionary poem. The third Voyage
takes the form of a meditative poem, the fourth misuses
words in its struggle for originality, and the fifth, on the
failure of vision, says what other poems by Crane have said
better.

But "Voyages VI," continuing the theme of the loss of
vision, with the "imaged Word" taking its place and with the
movement of the poem dependent rather more on its mythic
references than on its insistent visual images, is surely one of
Crane's greatest triumphs. Expressing its theme of the need
to move beyond the literally seen to the unseen in both visual
and mythic terms, its "blind seer"—like Arnold's "Blind Orion, hungry for the dawn"—can hope that his vision may be
restored if, like the Orion of Greek myth, he enters the sea
and swims toward Eos, goddess of the dawn. The "imaged
Word" of the last stanza will be what Crane will try to create
in *The Bridge*, but here it is enough that it is half-remembered,
half-imagined, heard only near Belle Isle, a curiously named
island, bleak and cold, in the straits of Belle Isle near New-
foundland, with its permanently ice-covered interior. If Word
and image should prove to be "cognate" with "Creation's

blithe and petalled word," perhaps it would be another *fiat lux*—"Let there be light"—even while remaining the poet's own creation.

"Voyages," uneven as the series is, contains Crane's greatest writing before *The Bridge*. The Bible, Greek myth, and Jung are all helpful in explicating the packed allusions in "Voyages VI," as well of course as Arnold's poems and Crane's own "North Labrador" and "Repose of Rivers," some of the chief images of which it picks up and repeats in its unparaphrasable concluding stanzas. What the poet hopes to hear is

> Creation's blithe and petalled word
> To the lounged goddess when she rose
> Conceding dialogue with eyes
> That smile unsearchable repose—
>
> Still fervid covenant, Belle Isle,
> —Unfolded floating dais before
> Which rainbows twine continual hair—
> Belle Isle, white echo of the oar!
>
> The imaged Word, it is, that holds
> Hushed willows anchored in its glow.
> It is the unbetrayable reply
> Whose accent no farewell can know.

What he awaits, I take it, is the word once spoken and now needed to be spoken again in a new idiom.

But if "Voyages VI" leads us to expect that Crane, like Whitman before him, will attempt to create a "new Bible," the series as a whole should also make us suspect that the effort will fail, for Whitman in his greatest visionary poems, not feeling himself either "derelict" or "blinded," could believe that the seen contained sufficient clues to the unseen, when perceived truly. When he turned to myth, as for example in "Faces" and "A Sight in Camp," it was to living myth felt as truth, not myth known as myth. Eos and Orion are literary props to Crane, helpful to him in creating a poem, but Christ was a presence to Whitman.

★   ★   ★

Crane thought of himself as the inheritor of both Blake and Whitman, as he makes clear in "Modern Poetry" and in his letters, an inheritor whose proper work would be to achieve "the articulation of the contemporary human consciousness *sub specie aeternitatis*," with the aid of "a peculiar type of perception, capable of apprehending some absolute and timeless concept of the imagination."[4] But another poet, also a "visionary" of sorts, was more important to him than either Whitman or Blake in the shaping of his style: Arthur Rimbaud, the French Symbolist, who had felt he had to disorder the senses in order to achieve his illuminations.

For his understanding of Whitman, Crane was considerably indebted to Ouspensky, who thought that it was "the logic of ecstasy" that had enabled Whitman to achieve the "cosmic consciousness" first heralded by Bucke. For his understanding of Blake, he was indebted to Foster Damon's pioneering study, which had presented Blake as Seer and Prophet. His discovery of Rimbaud he owed to Eliot. All three poets, as he understood them, led him to hope, as he tells us in "General Aims and Theories," that by "using our 'real' world somewhat as a spring-board," he could achieve a poem that would be "at least a stab at truth," an evocation of "a state of consciousness, an 'innocence' (Blake) or absolute beauty. In this condition there may be discoverable under new forms certain spiritual illuminations, shining with a mo-

4 "Modern Poetry," in *Collected Poems*, 175, 178.

rality essentialized from experience directly, and not from previous precepts or preconceptions."[5]

What Crane seemed not to realize when he paired Whitman and Blake—and sometimes seemed to be thinking of Rimbaud, whom he once called "the last great poet of our civilization," as belonging in the same company—was the difference between the two older "visionaries." Whitman had not wanted to use the "real" as a mere "spring-board" into the absolute. Rather, he had hoped to see deeply enough and truly enough into the real that the earth itself, as perceived, would supply the right poetic word. Blake claimed that his "Milton" was the result of "immediate Dictation"—he himself being merely the "secretary" for the real authors, who were "in eternity"—and similarly, with the aid of Scripture, had seen angels in a tree and created new prophetic myths. But Crane felt highly insecure on his portion of the "springboard" and, experiencing no "dictation" and seeing no angels in a tree, he had only fleeting intuitions and words to fall back on. What the words had once meant was not the poet's concern. As he wrote to Waldo Frank, "the romantic attitude must at least have the background of an age of faith, whether approved or disproved no matter."[6]

Like the good late Symbolist he was, Crane depended finally on poetry itself to express and support an implicitly religious Vision, which would, he hoped, lead him "from time's realm," but he had to disorder the senses more and more to achieve the suspect epiphanies that always deserted him in the "secular light" of the new day. By thought and circumstance, he was farther from Whitman and closer to the

5 "General Aims and Theories," in Philip Horton, *Hart Crane: The Life of an American Poet* (New York, 1957), 326–27.
6 *Letters*, 260.

writers of dream allegories and the theosophists than he knew.

Still, temperament as well as poetic aims seemed to Crane to link them together in "the visionary company of love"—a phrase ambiguous enough to permit him to emphasize his kinship with Whitman and to ignore their differences. One great difference he seems to have kept out of consciousness was the way Whitman's dear love of comrades had found expression in his poetry while Crane's had not. But there was another, less private, reason for Crane's defensiveness about his feeling of fraternal kinship with Whitman: Whitman was so completely out of fashion that to admire his work seemed proof of naïveté. Over and over in his letters Crane repeated his admiration for the "in" poets, but Whitman was "out" and Crane had to try to explain, defensively, to Allen Tate what it was in Whitman's verse that he could admire.

Signs of defensiveness are not confined to the letters. In *The Bridge*, the "Word" is ostensibly, in context, the Revealed Word of Scripture, but the reader need only take such allusions as the one to Lazarus metaphorically to see that the Word is that of the poet. If he were charged with a sentimental nostalgia for a dead faith, Crane had the nineteenth-century idea of the poet as the true Messiah to fall back on in self-defense. He could answer that, like the French Symbolists before him, he had simply used religious allusions to enrich his poetry.

But if that were so, his poem gave no answer to *The Waste Land*, and his "Psalm of Cathay" was really a hymn to nothing. The oxymoronic style owed much to literary fashion, but both its roots and its implications lay deeper—in vision. Only the ability to experience, to "see," meaning could support an "intrinsic" myth in which the "seen," being "seen as," would lead naturally into "seeing that," into belief. Seeing only a broken world, he knew not what to believe. When he jumped from the ship into the sea, he was putting into action what his poetry had implied all along.

CHAPTER IV

William Carlos Williams

Naturalizing the Unearthly

Williams may be thought of as Crane's opposite number, Crane's antithesis as person and poet. Crane wanted to be a visionary poet and at times succeeded in achieving his aim. When he failed, it was partly because the "sensations of urban life" that he theoretically embraced and wanted to affirm, he emotionally rejected, partly because, as the inheritor of the Symbolist style, he often wrote in such a way that the images in his poetry seem to be pointing not so much to the things of our experience as to systems of thought and belief. "The logic of metaphor" has already interpreted them before we encounter them in the poem—interpreted, digested, and placed them in categories so that they "mean." The bridge and the tunnel are symbols of fitful illuminations in the general darkness. Despite his original hopes for *The Bridge*, only the blind seer achieves a vision that Crane and his reader can finally trust.

After his earliest poetry and before his latest, Williams seems to have thought he wanted nothing to do with anything "visionary." "Facts" were enough, and poems should be made of "particulars"—that is, of discrete facts. If he had ever been asked, he would presumably have associated the "visionary" with the romantic or with the religious perspective of Eliot, both of which he vehemently rejected. ("I wanted reality in my poetry.") His effort was to "naturalize" the "sacred" yellow flower that "cures" men and only then, when it was no longer "unearthly," to choose it as his own. "What is not now will never be," he thought: that's the *fact*, whether we like it or not. "Keep Christ out of this." Accept the ugly and the painful: "Poor / Hoboken. Poor sad / Eliot. Poor memory."[1] Drop "the Christian coin," with its emblems of

1 *The Collected Later Poems of William Carlos Williams* (Rev. ed.; New York, 1967), 101, 115. All quotations from Williams' work are from this

dove and sword, "to its grave" in the ocean. Very late in life, writing about Brueghel's painting of the Nativity, he seems a little nostalgic when he writes that "they had eyes for visions in those days," but the old assumption that visions are for dreamers or "believers," facts for realists like himself, is still apparent in the background, however much he might admire the painting. An "objectivist" could hardly be expected to think of himself as a "visionary." This is one of the implications of his lifelong slogan, "no ideas but in things": the "ideas" of the older poets whom he called "romantic" but might have called "visionary" did not seem to him to grow out of an honest and attentive look at "things."

★　★　★

Yet there are good reasons for associating Williams with the visionary company Crane hoped to join, reasons that are to be found not in his own "ideas"—which are very often either confused or self-contradictory or both at once—but in his best poems and in the general shape of his career. Even in his early "Imagist" phase, his attention to "things," including other people, is not "objective," or value-free, as Imagist theory would have it and he himself thought it was, but contains a value judgment: these details, these particulars, even when they are grotesque or apparently ugly, have intrinsic meaning and value that we should not simply accept but treasure. In no other way is Williams' kinship with Whitman so readily apparent as in this acceptance of the commonly rejected. But not just accepted, sought out for special attention: "Where shall I find you, / you my grotesque fellows?" "I

---

volume and from the following: *The Collected Earlier Poems* (New York. 1966); *Pictures from Brueghel and Other Poems* (New York, 1962); and *Paterson* (New York, 1963).

walk back streets / admiring the houses / of the very poor"—
admiring them apparently for some reason other than their
visual beauty, some reason that has more to do with insight
than with sight. Williams was never an aesthete, though he
sometimes in lectures and readings talked like one.

Though for many years Williams insisted, with the nonrepresentational painters of the time, that poetry is not
"about" anything but itself, that the technique of a work of
art is the *subject* of the work (the Hartpence story: "That,
Madam, is paint"), still it seems to me clear that the reason
we value his best poetry is that it is indeed "about" something: about the "poetry" to be found in the common life.
Carrying on the legacy of Wordsworth and Whitman—without, for most of his life, apparently knowing it—he sought
out and celebrated the commonplace, the apparently unbeau-
tiful and unimportant, the "illegitimate things" that had not
before, he thought, entered poetry, except to be despised and
rejected.

Street sparrows and the old man gathering dog-lime in
the gutter seemed important enough to get his full attention:
"These things / astonish me beyond words." Driving along
the ugly street, he "saw," he tells us, "an elderly man," "a boy
of eight," and "a girl with one leg / over the rail of a balcony"
and was astonished at "the supreme importance / of this
nameless spectacle." And the spectacle need not have these
elements of potential human drama to seem to him of enormous importance:

> Between Walls
>
> the back wings
> of the
>
> hospital where
> nothing

will grow lie
cinders

in which shine
the broken

pieces of a green
bottle

Out of the context of *The Collected Earlier Poems*, this noncommittal poem might seem simply an example of imagist theory, and a better example than the more-often-cited "The Red Wheelbarrow" since it contains no editorializing, but in context it becomes an affirmation of the kind of beauty that may be found in the most unlikely place. More commonly, though, Williams is not content to leave the celebration merely implicit. "Sparrow Among Dry Leaves" concludes with a statement of the meaning he found as he watched the "hardly seen" sparrows eating, half-covered by dry leaves beside the iron fence: "hardly seen," but seen well enough to suggest "love's / obscure and insatiable / appetite." Or again, celebrating the hardy common roadside chicory and daisies, he could be moved to apparent overstatement as he tells us how much depends on our ability to see them as they are and what it means that they survive in the dryness:

The earth cracks and
is shriveled up;
the wind moans piteously;
the sky goes out
if you should fail.

However often he might repeat the Modernist dogma that poetry is about poetry only, he could write in "Illegitimate Things" that even in wartime poems could remind us that "water still flows— / The thrush still sings" despite the sound of distant gunfire, for "poems still conserve / the lan-

guage / of old ecstasies." In situation and thrust, this poem
might remind us of Whitman's "Cavalry Crossing a Ford,"
though Whitman felt there was no reason to call the implications he saw in what he so carefully described "illegitimate." Despite their metaphysical differences, the two poets
unite in seeking out the values of the common life that the
poet perceives and poems preserve.

Again, like Whitman and like all of our visionary poets,
Williams found support for his affirmations not so much in
"society" or culture as in "nature." (He carries this tendency
even further than Whitman, who was sometimes cheered by
thoughts of our "Manifest Destiny" or the promise of "one
world" contained in technology.) Both poets lived their lives
in cities and wrote as urban poets, but both found their chief
support in the natural, taking full advantage of the ambiguity
of that word that allows it to include the human as well as the
nonhuman. When Whitman was troubled by thoughts of
death in two of his greatest poems, "Out of the Cradle" and
"Lilacs," it was birdsong translated that comforted him. Although Williams found the song of the nightingale (*The Waste
Land*) and the hermit thrush ("Lilacs") too "romantic"—and
besides, quite outside his own experience—still a surprising
number of birds were apparently to be seen and heard in
industrial northern New Jersey if we follow the evidence of
his collected poems—or else Williams was especially on the
lookout for those that could be seen. In addition to the expected sparrows, robins, chickadees, gulls, and starlings, we
find orioles, brown thrashers, cardinals, wood thrushes (they
like suburbs), woodpeckers, and others, with the commonest
most highly valued. This attention to nature in the sense of
the prehuman or nonhuman in Williams' poems includes the
seasons, moon and stars, the weather, trees, and the common
flowers, with special attention to those too common to be

widely admired, or perhaps even noticed, like Queen Anne's lace and mullein.

This aspect of Williams' work—his tendency always to value the "natural" over the "civilized," cultured, sophisticated, or "refined"—inevitably reminds us of Whitman. Whitman had said he could turn and live with the animals, and Williams seemed always especially attracted to the poor, the ignorant, the despised, to those who were "natural" because they were outside the dominant culture. Whitman had thought the scent of his armpits aroma finer than prayer, and Williams, noting that he seemed to want to have "a part in everything," acknowledged the importance to him of smell. No Prufrock he, with his delight in tasting and smelling everything, even the "rank" odors of spring. Whatever was "natural" must have value—an idea that could contribute to his late effort to compose "the music of survival" but could also lead him at times into the sentimentality and anti-intellectualism that weaken so many of his poems.

★ ★ ★

Most of the disappointingly small number of really memorable poems to be found scattered here and there among the poems Williams decided to preserve in *The Collected Earlier Poems*, *The Collected Later Poems*, *Paterson* (all five books, as completed), and *Pictures from Brueghel* may be called at least implicitly "visionary" as I have been using that word, and the best of them are visionary formally as well as thematically. I shall treat here just three of the shorter poems and the late masterpiece "Desert Music." I have commented on the first three before, in *American Poets*, and have not changed my mind about what I said about them there, so some repetition is no doubt inevitable, but here I want to look more closely at why we should describe them as "visionary" poems.

In the familiar first section of *Spring and All*, Williams

counters the "alien universe" and "dead nature" notions that haunted so many of his contemporaries—and not just Robinson and Frost, Jeffers and Aiken. Drawing on both what can be seen and what can't be seen but is known, he finds life and value implicit in nature, thus lining up with Whitman and against Stevens and Eliot:

> By the road to the contagious hospital
> under the surge of the blue
> mottled clouds driven from the
> northeast—a cold wind. Beyond, the
> waste of broad, muddy fields
> brown with dried weeds, standing and fallen
>
> patches of standing water
> the scattering of tall trees
>
> All along the road the reddish
> purplish, forked, upstanding, twiggy
> stuff of bushes and small trees
> with dead, brown leaves under them
> leafless vines—
>
> Lifeless in appearance, sluggish
> dazed spring approaches—
>
> They enter the new world naked,
> cold, uncertain of all
> save that they enter. All about them
> the cold, familiar wind—
>
> Now the grass, tomorrow
> the stiff curl of wildcarrot leaf
> One by one objects are defined—
> It quickens: clarity, outline of leaf
>
> But now the stark dignity of
> entrance—Still, the profound change

> has come upon them: rooted, they
> grip down and begin to awaken

The poem would not work as well as it does if its affirmation of life were an easy one. The scene is "lifeless in appearance," threatening, but what appears to the casual glance can be deceptive. The eye that sees with the aid of memory and thought sees beyond or through the apparent "waste land" with its dark clouds driven by the cold wind, the dead weeds, and the dead leaves. Taking its cue from the literally visible color in the bark of the bushes and twigs, the eye of the mind moves on to the perception of the analogy between vegetable and human birth. The analogy rests on the slightest of visual evidence, but that evidence is supported by memory of past springs and anticipation of what will happen in the days to come: "Now the grass, tomorrow" the common roadside flower wild carrot or Queen Anne's lace. Plants and persons alike enter "naked, cold, uncertain" and must grip down in the earth in which they are rooted if they are to awaken, now that "the profound change / has come upon them." Sight, memory, knowledge, and foresight work together in the poem to make interpretive vision possible.

But the unity of man and nature seen in this poem is not the whole picture in Williams' work. The distinction between living persons and the inanimate in nature is apparent to "the intelligent eye" with careful and patient observation of the explicit in "Fine Work with Pitch and Copper":

> Now they are resting
> in the fleckless light
> separately in unison
>
> like the sacks

of sifted stone stacked
regularly by twos

about the flat roof
ready after lunch
to be opened and strewn

The copper in eight
foot strips has been
beaten lengthwise

down the center at right
angles and lies ready
to edge the coping

One still chewing
picks up a copper strip
and runs his eye along it

What is first seen is the superficial similarity between the resting roofers and the sacks of stone, but then the men get to work again and the difference becomes apparent. The men are artists in their own way as the poet himself is, they making a roof, he a poem. Such making requires judgment and careful use of the eye. A merely biological or physical perspective would reveal an identity between the sacks and the men that the poet's vision reveals as incomplete: sacks of sifted stone do not create either roofs or poems. Man is a distinctive part of nature, as the poet or artist can see.

"A Unison" adds a further dimension to what is revealed by sight and insight in "Spring and All" and "Fine Work," an obscure sense of the "sacred" and "the Undying":

The grass is very green, my friend,
and tousled, like the head of—
your grandson, yes? And the mountain,

the mountain we climbed
twenty years since for the last
time (I write this thinking
of you) is saw-horned as then
upon the sky's edge—an old barn
is peaked there also, fatefully,
against the sky. And there it is
and we can't shift it or change
it or parse it or alter it
in any way. Listen! Do you not hear
them? the singing? There it is and
we'd better acknowledge it and
write it down that way, not otherwise.
Not twist the words to mean
what we should have said but to mean
—what cannot be escaped: the
mountain riding the afternoon as
it does, the grass matted green,
green underfoot and the air—
rotten wood. Hear! Hear them!
the Undying. The hill slopes away,
then rises in the middleground,
you remember, with a grove of gnarled
maples centering the bare pasture,
sacred, surely—for what reason?
I cannot say. Idyllic!
a shrine cinctured there by
the trees, a certainty of music!
a unison and a dance, joined
at this death's festival: Something
of a shed snake's skin, the beginning
goldenrod. Or, best, a white stone,
you have seen it: *Mathilda Maria*
Fox—and near the ground's lip,

all but undecipherable, *Aet Suae,*
Anno 9—still there, the grass
dripping of last night's rain—and
welcome! The thin air, the near,
clear brook water!—and could not,
and died, unable; to escape
what the air and the wet grass—
through which, tomorrow, bejeweled,
the great sun will rise—the
unchanging mountains, forced on them—
and they received, willingly!
Stones, stones of a difference
joining the others at pace. Hear!
Hear the unison of their voices. . . .

The religious affirmation implied here rests on no clear visible evidence at all, on what seems no more than an "intimation" that draws Williams in this poem nearly as close to Wordsworth as it does to Whitman. These things are "sacred, surely," but "for what reason? / I cannot say." There is only the

certainty of music!
a unison and a dance, joined
at this death's festival.

With the distinction between the animate and the inanimate now obscured or transcended, as it had been for Whitman so often and as laboratory scientists are more and more finding it these days, all nature, the whole cosmos, can seem to be singing in celebration of life. The "Deep Religious Faith" of which Williams wrote in the poem of that title in *The Desert Music* has here driven him "beyond the remote borders of poetry itself," to say nothing of the evidence of the literally seen or perceived. Williams never wrote a more obviously "visionary" poem or one so closely related to a long tradition.

"The Desert Music," a longer and more thoughtful visionary poem celebrating "the music of survival," is surely one of Williams' finest. But perhaps just because it is more "thoughtful" than "A Unison," it is more ambiguous in its meaning and more careless in its diction. Formally, there is no question about its fitting the visionary paradigm. As the poet and his wife wander in and out of places of entertainment and through the streets, the poem seems to move in and out of the mind of the poet, who is noting the motionless fetal form on the bridge and the dancing and the insistent Latin-American music in the cafés, remembering and thinking about the sensations of the train journey across the desert, the purposes of poetry, and the poet's problem of getting the true music, which can be heard only in the mind, into his poem somehow.

The "dance" of the poem begins and ends with a fetal form, the one dimly seen on the bridge (lifeless or just drunk?) and the infant in the womb before birth, but whether the form is really there or merely imagined is open to some question. "Only the poem! / Only the made poem, the verb calls it into being," the poet thinks at one point. (Normally, the expression "to call into being" would mean "to create," not to "discover.") The half-seen, perhaps lifeless form on the bridge, which by its fetal position suggests the promise of new life and the nature of the true music, merges with half-heard true music itself, and both seem to be questioned at times by the prose part of the poet's mind:

> In the street it hit
> me in the face as we started to walk again. Or
> am I merely playing the poet? Do I merely invent
> it out of whole cloth? I thought

In contrast with this uncertainty, there is no question about the existence of "the lying music" to be heard at all times, inside and outside the cafés. However false, it cannot help but be *heard*; there is no need to wonder whether it is merely imagined:

> Why don't these Indians get over this nauseating
> prattle about their souls and their loves and sing
> us something else for a change?

"But there is another music," and it is that music that is affirmed as real as the poem ends. The "lying music" is forgotten now:

> But what's THAT?
>
>   the music! the
> *music!* as when Casals struck
> and held a deep cello tone
> and I am speechless

But not totally speechless for long, as memory conflates the mysterious shape on the bridge and the many births at which the poet-physician has assisted:

> a child in the womb prepared to imitate life,
> warding its life against
> a birth of awful promise. The music
> guards it, a mucus, a film that surrounds it,
> a benumbing ink that stains the
> sea of our minds—to hold us off—shed
> of a shape close as it can get to no shape,
> a music! a protecting music

At this stage in his career, Williams seems well beyond his Imagist-Objectivist phase, in which so much—everything, really—depended on full attentiveness and accurate observation of the sensed world outside the mind. The poem

ends with the false music no longer heard and the true music
no longer questioned:

> And I could not help thinking
> of the wonders of the brain that
> hears that music and of our
> skill sometimes to record it.

★   ★   ★

The failure of *Paterson* as a coherent long poem could have
been anticipated by any thoughtful reader who had followed
Williams' long career carefully, but if it had not been anticipated before Book I came out, the Author's Note or "Argument" included with the first book should have aroused anxiety among the poet's admirers. For there, the poet who had
for so long insisted that there are "no ideas but in things,"
that "things" must be allowed to speak for themselves, not
forced into any preconceived patterns of belief, wrote that

Paterson is a long poem in four parts—that a man in himself is a city,
beginning, seeking, achieving and concluding his life in ways which
the various aspects of a city may embody—if imaginatively conceived—any city, all the details of which may be made to voice his
most intimate convictions. Part One introduces the elemental character of the place. The Second Part comprises the modern replicas.
Three will seek a language to make them vocal, and Four, the river
below the falls, will be reminiscent of episodes—all that any one
man may achieve in a lifetime.

A city's "details . . . *may be made to voice*" the poet's "convictions." Just so London life had been made to voice Eliot's
private convictions in *The Waste Land*, which Williams had
devoted a career to trying to answer. Did the poet feel free to
force "things" into a pattern of belief? Whatever it might turn
out to be, apparently, *Paterson* would not be consistently guided
by the caution expressed in "A Unison" in the lines,

> . . . . And there it is
> and we can't shift it or change
> it or parse it or alter it
> in any way. . . .

Even if we suppose that by "may be made to voice" Williams really meant "may be perceived as voicing," we are left with a muddle, for he had always insisted, in his verse and out of it, that preconceived ideas or "convictions"—beliefs—should not precede but follow attention.

When the poem as planned, in four books, was completed, the poet's friends and supporters would find they had another shock coming to them: Book IV not only did not "answer" Eliot but seemed to confirm his evaluation of the waste land of modern urban life. After imitating the form and substance of the "low life" section of "A Game of Chess" in *The Waste Land*, the poet turned back to the way things— the river and the life around it—had been in the good old days, before the pollution had entered the river, and the society along its banks, and the river itself had been sucked into "the sea that sucks in all rivers." Book IV ends in nostalgia for a lost simplicity, beauty, purity—no proper answer to *The Waste Land* surely; a confirmation rather, if anything.

The "answer" to Eliot had to wait for Book V, added after the poet had become aware of why the original *Paterson* had disappointed his friends. Echoing the detested poem, especially the "Death by Water" section ("Gentile or Jew," "the sea is not our home"), the poet insists now that the proper work of the artist is not to let "things" speak to him and make his art true to them but to *create* a world of his own: "Pollock's blobs of paint. . . . Nothing else is real." But then, adding to the difficulty of understanding how this conviction fits with "no ideas but in things"—the slogan that has been repeated in the poem—in a comment on a painting of the Nativity we read that "they had eyes for visions in those days." Whether this should be taken to mean that "vision" (in the context, clearly desirable) is impossible in this age, when the river has first become polluted and then entered the ultimate pollution, or impossible in the poet's old age, is far from clear.

In any case, if the "measure" (of the poem) is "all we know" and beyond the work of art "nothing else is real," including the "field of flowers" that has just been celebrated, it is hard to see how even the afterthought of Book V, added to clarify the originally intended meaning of the poem, can be interpreted as an answer to Eliot's poem. But if it is no answer logically, Williams tried hard to make it one emotionally by ending the new book on a positive note, even though to do so required turning away from present things to describe old paintings and tapestries, "recalling the Jew," quoting from the New Testament, and confessing that "dreams possess me." The meaning of the poem that we should like to remember had come earlier, in Book III, and seems now to have been forgotten: "Sing me a song to make death tolerable, a song / of a man and a woman"—a man and a woman in the present:

> The riddle of a man and a woman
>
> For what is there but love, that stares death
> in the eye, love, begetting marriage—
> not infamy, not death

★   ★   ★

"Asphodel, That Greeny Flower," Williams' last long poem, first collected in *Pictures from Brueghel and Other Poems* just a year before his death, could be called a "visionary" poem only if we were to replace the visual base of "vision" with memory and imagination. Facing death himself after several strokes, Williams turned away from chicory and daisies to the flower of classical legend supposed to grace the Elysian fields of all the dead. The poem as a whole, and especially the "Coda," is not an exercise in vision as Williams had always tried to practice it but a summing up of a career and a life, a plea for forgiveness and an affirmation of love for Flossie, and a final statement of faith. It seems to me one of Williams' finest poems, but it has to be judged in its own terms, not in terms of either his earlier practice or his earlier, too often insisted upon, "theory."

For by now Williams is not just beyond his Imagist and Objectivist phases but beyond the kind of visionary poem he had written in "Desert Music." If there is still any sense in the old slogan "no ideas but in things," the sense has been radically changed, for the "things" are now remembered things, "pressed flowers" in the book of memory, or imagined flowers like the asphodel itself. Book III of the poem is "dedicated in the imagination / to memory / of the dead," and the imagination no longer stands in contrast with the "facts" that we must be true to:

                                    Don't think
          that because I say this
                    in a poem
                              it can be treated lightly
          or that the facts will not uphold it.
                    Are facts not flowers
                              and flowers facts
          or poems flowers
                    or all works of the imagination,
                              interchangeable?

The "Coda" of "Asphodel" is Williams' testament of

faith, his version of that "deep religious faith" he had written of: "Inseparable from the fire / its light / takes precedence over it. . . . the heat will not overtake the light. / That's sure." "Imagination" no longer has reference only, or even chiefly, to the aesthetic, whether "Pollock's blobs of paint" or old poems, but has become openly noetic and redemptive: "love and imagination / are of a piece," and we are "secure, / by grace of the imagination, / safe in its care."

The whole poem, the "Coda" tells us, should be read as a "celebration of the light," which should be understood as inseparable from imagination and love:

> Light, the imagination
> and love,
>   in our age,
> by natural law,
>   which we worship,
>   maintain
> all of a piece
>   their dominance.

Whether consciously or not, Williams seems in these passages to be making peace at last with his old enemy Eliot, especially when, after referring to the many different ways of celebrating the light, he quotes Eliot quoting Spenser's wedding song—"Sweet Thames, run softly." Eliot's way of waiting for the time when "the fire and the rose" would be known as "one" is not Williams' way, presumably because he thinks it not true to "our age" or "natural law," but the weddings celebrated by the two poets have much in common. The "summer lightning" is seen before it is felt, but if the light is first, it is also last:

> For our wedding, too,
>   the light was wakened
>   and shone. The light!

                    the light stood before us
                                waiting!
                                        I thought the world
            stood still.

The light experienced at the time of the wedding and
now remembered is not to be sharply distinguished from the
light of the summer lightning with which the "Coda" opens
and which is followed by "what we have dreaded," but the
source now is the sun itself, not a momentary flash:

                        In the huge gap
                                between the flash
                and the thunderstroke
                        spring has come in
                                or a deep snow fallen.

But there is a distinction of a sort: the "huge gap" was more
imagined or felt than "real," but the troubled years of the
long marriage were lived, not imagined, though it takes love
and imagination working together to heal the memories. Old
age still provides "an eternity" in which to "laugh and play."

                    If a man die
                                it is because death
                                    has first
                    possessed his imagination.

Whether or not Williams was conscious of it as he wrote,
he was closer in "Asphodel" not only to the Eliot of *The Four
Quartets* but to Whitman in old age. The Darwin and Columbus passages in the poem—voyages of discovery, both—remind us of parts of "Passage to India," and the "Coda" seems
quite close in spirit, without in any way seeming to echo,
Whitman's "Grand Is the Seen." Like Whitman before him,

Williams had said over and over, in effect, "down with priest-craft," but he ends beyond doctrinal differences. Whitman's poems of old age and Williams' have much in common, even though "in our age" there is "the bomb" to make us "come to our deaths in silence."

But as a poet at any rate Williams did not go to his death in silence but in a song celebrating the flower that makes death tolerable:

>   Asphodel
>   has no odor
>   save to the imagination
>   but it too
>   celebrates the light.
>   It is late
>   but an odor
>   as from our wedding
>   has revived for me
>   and begun again to penetrate
>   into all crevices
>   of my world.

★   ★   ★

Despite the fact that Williams wrote too much (or at least preserved too much, with an almost total lack of self-criticism) and too carelessly; despite the fact that he often seems more familiar with the things he is treating than with the history and implications of the words he is using to speak of the things; despite his anti-intellectualism—as when he attacks James, Dewey, and Whitehead without, clearly, knowing much about them—and his quite-frequent senti-mentality, which are not unconnected; despite too the con-fused and often self-contradictory "theories" on which he seemed to pride himself—which might be called expressions of an attitude, so far as they are self-consistent—despite all this and more, Williams in his best work came closer to reclaiming Whitman's vision for a later age than Crane had.

True, his early work is generally only "proto-visionary," with the visionary aspects of the visual only implicit. True also, when, as in "Asphodel, That Greeny Flower" and other late poems, the visionary becomes explicit, he is no longer looking at chicory and daisies or the houses of the poor but contemplating the meaning of his long "journey to love" and the power of the poet to discover and of the poem to preserve the values we must live by. But he did write enough fully realized visionary poems that fit the Whitman paradigm to fill a respectable volume even if, by a strict accounting, we have to rule "Asphodel" out. "Desert Music" may be a flawed poem, but it seems to me still a great poem in the visionary mode.

He wrote these visionary poems apparently forgetting his constantly restated mature conviction that the subject-matter of poetry is only poetry, so that the purpose of technique must be to call attention to itself. But I suspect that the Hartpence story he kept repeating late in life to lecture audiences did not strike him as meaning that. For poetry to be about poetry meant for it to be about life, or at least about what's really important in life. This is clearer in his verse than in his prose opinions. His verse often seems to express the values he lived by better than he knew, as in the following lines from "Deep Religious Faith," which certainly do not suggest that poetry is only about poetry:

> Shame on our poets,
> They have caught the prevalent fever:
> impressed
> by the "laboratory,"
> they have forgot

> the flower!
>   which goes beyond all
>   laboratories!

Williams' best poems succeed so wonderfully in perceiving and celebrating light, love, and the noetic power of the poetic imagination that they make his prose opinions seem irrelevant. He shows that Hart Crane's ultimate failure to reclaim anything like Whitman's vision was not inevitable either in northern New Jersey or in the desert of the Southwest, even in the time of "the bomb."

A poet in the Emerson-Whitman tradition of the poet as "seer," Williams had less skill with words than Crane but a clearer, less defensive vision of people and things. Perhaps he was just a more fortunate man? At any rate, his best poetry illustrates the at-least-partial truth in Emerson's conviction, expressed in "The Poet," that it is not meter but meter-making argument that distinguishes the important poet from the little versifiers. That this is a typically "romantic" idea is clear, just as Williams' determination not to be guilty of romanticism is also clear.

Should we say then that Williams was, at least at times—and I should say at his best—a "visionary poet" despite himself, or at least despite the intellectual part of himself?

CHAPTER V

Theodore Roethke

Learning to See in the Dark

Very late in his career, in "The Abyss," Roethke followed Crane's example by invoking Whitman's aid, writing "Be with me, Walt Whitman, maker of catalogues." To a poet who had written in his Notebook a few years earlier that "the recovery of things is our business: See! we're blessed by what we see!" and "I wish I could find an event that meant as much as simple seeing!" calling Whitman a "maker of catalogues" would not seem faint praise.[1]

The lateness of the public acknowledgment seems to have had nothing to do with an "anxiety of influence." Roethke's early favorites had simply never included Whitman. The late Yeats, Blake, Christopher Smart, the Elizabethan and Metaphysical lyricists—these had been his favorites, not Whitman, so that when we find Whitman mentioned for the first time in *Straw for the Fire* in a passage written late in the poet's life—"Nietzsche and Whitman my fathers: and yet I cannot worship power. I hate power. I reject it"—the notation takes us by surprise and has the appearance of being a recent discovery of Roethke's own.[2]

But whether Roethke had known it for some time or was just discovering it, the kinship here acknowledged by "father" was, and had long been, real. Similarities only faintly suggested in *Open House* become apparent when we put the whole body of work of the two poets side by side. Both move from finding the visionary implicit in the visible to the suspicion that at times "the visible obscures" and the "Unseen" is "grander" than the seen. Both make use of archetypal images without appearing to write as Symbolists. Both also

---

1 *Straw for the Fire: From the Notebooks of Theodore Roethke*, ed. David Wagoner (New York, 1974), 217.
2 *Ibid.*, 230.

celebrate a self in the process of being discovered and achieved. And both pose as "roughs" who despise the genteel, indulge a taste for the vulgar, write their "autobiography in colossal cipher," and make poetry out of the "shameful"—Whitman's "lovers" holding his hand, Roethke's allusions to autoeroticism.

Of course, the differences between them are many, obvious, and both personal and historical. Roethke's manic-depressive affliction, with his periodic breakdowns, must have been very much harder to bear than Whitman's partial suppression of his homoerotic impulses. And he lived in a darker century, when not just the doctrines of the organized churches but all religious or otherwise supportive beliefs had been or were being undermined, so that much of the time he could only think of himself not as a "blind seer" but "an eyeless starer." Then, too, with what seems to have been good reason, he had a personal sense of sin, or guilt, that partly prompted and partly directed what he called his "long journey out of the self"—a passage that Whitman in his own way also accomplished, I suspect, but without making his dark times the subject of his published work.

Still, for all their differences, Roethke remains Whitman's chief successor after Williams, and in some important ways more truly Whitman's heir than Williams was without knowing it, or Hart Crane, who aspired to be. I suspect he was helped, not hindered, toward his achievement by having no conscious desire to carry on Whitman's work for a later time.

★ ★ ★

Although Roethke's major contribution to the visionary tradition in American poetry would not begin until the poems in *The Lost Son, Open House* (1941), his first volume, contained some strong suggestions, as hindsight enables us to see, of the post-Modernist, romantic-visionary direction in which he would soon move. While other young poets of his generation were mastering the idiom called for by critics who had learned what to expect of poetry from *The Waste Land*, Roethke could ignore Eliot's call for impersonal poetry, with the poet himself hidden behind masks and *personnae*, his "mythic method," and his rejection of the Romantics, and write in the title poem of his collection that

> My secrets cry aloud.
> I have no need for tongue.
> My heart keeps open house,
> My doors are widely swung.
> An epic of the eyes
> My love, with no disguise.
>
> ....
>
> Myself is what I wear:
> I keep the spirit spare.[3]

"Prayer" and "The Signals," which he placed together in the volume, foreshadow what would become a major preoccupation—discovering the self by learning to see the world around him in depth. The witty neo-Metaphysical style and the tongue-in-cheek tone in which the eye is chosen over the other sense organs in "Prayer" will not mislead those who have followed the career to the end:

> If I must of my Senses lose,
> I pray Thee, Lord, that I may choose
> Which of the Five I shall retain
> Before oblivion clouds the brain.
>
> ....
>
> Let Light attend me to the grave!

3   *The Collected Poems of Theodore Roethke* (New York, 1966), 3. All subsequent quotations from Roethke's verse are from this edition.

"The Signals" then clarifies the visionary second meaning of "Light":

> Often I meet, on walking from a door,
> A flash of objects never seen before.
>
> As known particulars come wheeling by,
> They dart across a corner of the eye.
>
> They flicker faster than a blue-tailed swift,
> Or when dark follows dark in lightning rift.
>
> They slip between the fingers of my sight.
> I cannot put my glance upon them tight.
>
> Sometimes the blood is privileged to guess
> The things the eye or hand cannot possess.

Such an interpretation of "vision," allowing for the "dawning" of an object on us, takes us well beyond Ezra Pound's "ideogrammatic method," with its implicit assumption that "facts speak for themselves," so that the simple mimetic image supplies all that is needed for its interpretation. It suggests rather the titles of some recent books describing vision research—Kaufman's *Sight and Mind*, for instance, or his *Perception: The World Transformed*, or Gregory's *The Intelligent Eye*, or Frisby's *Seeing: Illusion, Brain, and Mind*. Or if, as is rather more likely, the poem's last lines should suggest D. H. Lawrence to us, they do so without betraying the legacy of early Whitman, for whom perception was also a function of the whole body, as it is for Roethke in the poem with which he chose to end his volume, "Night Journey," which takes Emerson's "invulnerable" poet-Seer-celebrator and Whitman's poet of the Open Road on a darker journey toward a similar end:

> Now as the train bears west,
> Its rhythm rocks the earth,

> And from my Pullman berth
> I stare into the night
> While others take their rest.
> Bridges of iron lace,
> A suddenness of trees,
> A lap of mountain mist
> All cross my line of sight,
> Then a bleak wasted place,
> And a lake below my knees.
> Full on my neck I feel
> The straining at a curve;
> My muscles move with steel,
> I wake in every nerve.
>
> ....
> I stay up half the night
> To see the land I love.

Although the cadences here could hardly be less Whitmanic, and the train ride through the night suggests Frost's
"Desert Places" more than Whitman's "Song of the Open
Road," the thematic movement in the poem from the "star-
ing" of the fourth line to the metaphoric, even implicitly
kinesthetic perception carried by "see" in the last continues
the idea of the poet's role announced by Emerson and prac-
ticed by Whitman. The "seeing" that the poet hopes to
achieve here is highly personal and subjective, but at the same
time "open" to let the world in, not just through a "transparent eyeball" but with all the body's capacity to perceive: the
poet in the world, responding to the world, and in responding, finding it meaningful. There is no suggestion here of
Crane's straining beyond the personal with the help of myth.
The poet for whom the position of the lake was perceived as
below his knees would soon explore the doubleness of things

in the greenhouse poems, which lift the uniquely subjective and personal to the archetypal, find the "self" by doing full justice to the real "other," in the process transforming the personal into the universal. Crane's experience had taught him to distrust the self. Williams in his Imagist phase had often seemed to be saying that passive attentiveness was enough. Although the poet of *Open House* has not yet really found his own voice and his own best subjects, there is evidence in these poems of the direction in which he would soon move: toward finding a self by recalling the world of childhood.

★   ★   ★

The Lost Son opens with two poems that may be read as exemplifying the kind of "seeing" wished for in "The Signals" and partially suggested in "Night Journey." "Cuttings" and "Cuttings (later)" begin with the literally seen, move quickly to the known but out of sight, and end, in the second poem, with both imaginative and sensuous empathic response, expressing the vision in a poetic form shaped by what is seen, literally and imaginatively, so that they may be called Roethke's first fully visionary poems. In the abstract terms of paraphrase, the vision in them is that of the kinship of all life as the living creatures struggle to survive and grow, the common struggle binding together the slips, the speaker, and finally, in the second poem, the saints whom the speaker has been led to think of. The movement of the two poems parallels that in Whitman's "A Noiseless, Patient Spider."

The slips that have been cut and stuck in moist loam to start new plants are first seen in "objective," purely visual terms as objects outside the speaker and wholly other, "sticks" on which the "stem-fur dries" as they "droop," cut off from life-giving moisture. But then past experience of other cuttings seen in the greenhouse and mature biological knowledge of how osmosis works come to the aid of the eye. Activities too slow to be seen and changes too gradual to be registered by any single visual image and so known only with the help of memory have thus to be "imagined." That they are truly imagined, not invented, is confirmed in any elementary biology course that takes up such facts common to "higher" and "lower" forms of life as osmosis and cell structure and growth. "Nudges" and "coaxing" can express in human terms the speaker's sense of identification with the barely living sticks without being a "poetic conceit" such as "the heavens wept."

In "Cuttings (later)" the slips are known to be putting down roots and expected to survive by a process now viewed as holy or sacred—"resurrection," "saint." Perception now has become wholly metaphoric, allowing the speaker to "hear" with the mind's ear the inaudible and "feel" in his own body the moisture necessary for life on whatever level. Sexual images in the last lines complete the identification begun in the second stanza of the first poem. Read together, the two poems can be thought of as a single visionary poem dramatizing a kind of I-Thou dialogue with objects at once very foreign and very familiar to the son of a greenhouse keeper.

In these, "Root Cellar," and the other greenhouse poems, Roethke learned in effect that he could follow Emerson's advice to poets to write their "autobiography in colossal cipher," using memory in such a way that the private would become representative. (Late in his career as a lyric poet, Eliot, perhaps surprisingly, had seemed to agree, writing in "A Note on War Poetry," that "private experience at its greatest intensity / Becoming universal . . . we call 'poetry.'") In the greenhouse world of childhood memory, all the most important discoveries were waiting to be made, needing only to be consciously recalled, reflected on, and interpreted, as Whitman had in "Out of the Cradle" and "There Was a Child Went Forth."

The world recalled was not idealized. It was not safe, or painless, or unambiguous in its meaning. In it, the visible reveals, but what it reveals is the familiar mixture of good and evil, beauty and ugliness, life and death. In it, the orchids in the greenhouse may appear to be "adder-mouthed" and may be seen as "devouring infants." The child pulling weeds "under the concrete benches" where "lewd monkey-tails" hang feels as if he were "crawling on all fours, / Alive, in a slippery grave." In the root cellar, roots dangle and droop "obscenely" from "mildewed crates," making "a congress of stinks." In the "forcing house," life in the form of "scums, mildews, smuts" flourishes on the nourishment provided by "dung and ground bones."

In some of the greenhouse poems, the images of the visible and otherwise perceptible world are followed by what amounts to an abstractly expressed interpetation, as they are in "Root Cellar" by "nothing would give up life: / Even the dirt kept breathing a small breath" and in "Moss Gathering" by "I always felt. . . . / As if I had committed, against the whole scheme of life, a desecration," but in others the meaning is wholly implicit in the archetypal associations of the images themselves. "Big Wind" seems to me perhaps the most memorable of the poems in which the images do not lead to but contain their meaning. In it, the greenhouse becomes for the speaker a ship weathering a storm at sea and then finally, as the ship-in-a-storm suggestions point beyond themselves to another crisis situation, the planet sailing through the cosmic winds of "empty" space. The poem presents in larger terms the conflict that had been presented in miniature in "Cuttings" and "Root Cellar": the danger, the

threats, the precariousness, and the promise implicit in the
situation of all living things. Life and death now seem pitted
against each other in fierce open combat, not quietly as in
"Cuttings" or ambiguously as in "Root Cellar," but with dramatic clarity, so that when the storm dies down and the
greenhouse, still intact, sails safely into "the calm morning, /
Carrying her full cargo of roses," the affirmation suggested
by the image of a ship reaching port is unqualified.

The hope of survival had been tested many times before
and would be again, over and over throughout Roethke's
career, but the final lines of "Big Wind" prepare us for the
ending of this section of the volume, with the "dying" and
"newly dead" flowers of "Flower Dump" preceded by the
adventure of the child on top of the greenhouse and followed,
in the last lines of "Carnations," by the vision of the "clear
autumnal weather of eternity" in a "windless perpetual
morning." That the overtly religious language here has been
poetically earned, not just willed or tacked on, is suggested
by the parallel that has been visually discovered in "Transplanting" between the "turning and tamping" of the hands of
the worker and the "stretching and reaching" of the flower as
it seeks light and air. "Transplanting" might be misread as a
merely descriptive "Imagist" poem if it were not followed
immediately by the metaphoric stretching and reaching of
the child on top of the greenhouse, by the multiple deaths in
"Flower Dump," and by the religious vocabulary of "Carnations."

The Lost Son, in short, opens with a group of visionary
poems of a kind that had never been written before, with life
and death so intricately intermingled and delicately balanced
at the very center of childhood experience.

★   ★   ★

The next section begins with a poem that may serve to remind us that any discovered analogy between Roethke's treatment of childhood and Whitman's must not be pressed too far. In "Night Crow," the darkness that Whitman's child on the beach had discovered in the song of the thrush and the sound of the surf is found to exist within the self, not just in the outer world:

> When I saw that clumsy crow
> Flap from a wasted tree,
> A shape in the mind rose up:
> Over the gulfs of dream
> Flew a tremendous bird
> Further and further away
> Into a moonless black,
> Deep in the brain, far back.

Though this frightening discovery is balanced in the later poems that make up the section—with "The Minimal" bringing the realization of the "healing" accomplished by "bacterial creepers / Wriggling through wounds," "The Cycle" revealing the "dark water, underground" rising as mist toward the sun, to fall again as rain, and "The Waking" describing the feeling of kinship with nature once experienced on an early morning walk—still the darker opening poem effectively dominates the section and seems to lead directly into the title poem of the volume, which opens the final section. For "The Lost Son" is first and most clearly a poem about a psychic breakdown and partial recovery. In it, the darkness and death are again internal and projected onto the world, the flight is from the deepest self, and the winter light that seems to await discovery in the final section must be found in the world outside the mind if it is to be trusted as real.

Although the work of the "mad" poets Christopher Smart and Blake, both favorites of Roethke's, may have helped to make "The Lost Son" possible, no poem really like this intensely mimetic rendering of the experience of fear, flight, and loss of control followed by the beginning of recovery had ever been written before, and none so great, to my knowledge, since. If we try to relate it to the visionary tradition that is my subject, two points seem worth mentioning. First, and most clearly, it reenacts the loss, and later the tentative hope of possible recovery, of the participatory vision, the feeling of "belonging," vaguely suggestive of "nature mysticism," that had been celebrated in the earlier poems in the volume. Second, the dominant images in "The Flight," "The Pit," and "The Gibber"—chiefly images of sound and touch and body-feeling—are felt as unquestionable in a way impossible for visual images to be, while "The Return" begins and ends with visual images ("The way to the boiler was dark . . . weeds / Moved in a slow up-sway"), and visual perception alone permits the hope of recovery of the healing vision not yet achieved in the final section, as the winter light reveals the "beautiful surviving bones" of dead weeds "swinging in the wind" and "light travelled over the wide field; / Stayed," so that "the mind moved, not alone."

Or seemed not to be. Could the experience be trusted to be real, not just imagined, as the speaker earlier had imagined the leaves mocking him? If visual perception necessarily required interpretation, can we be sure that what we think we see is "real," really *there*, and what it seems to be?

> Was it light?
> Was it light within?
> Was it light within light?
> Stillness becoming alive,
> Yet still?
>
> A lively understandable spirit

Once entertained you.
It will come again.
Be still.
Wait.

The recovery that can only be waited for in "The Lost
Son," after suffering that had both created the need for the
light and supplied the poetic means of making the hoped-for
return of vision believable, is completed in "A Field of
Light." The suffering that had been minutely acted out in the
earlier poem is foreshortened here, presented in images of
death, chill, and alienation in the first two sections, only to
be left behind in the beautifully moving last section, in which
the joyful discovery of participating in a meaningful process
is not stated but embodied in every aspect of the form. Just
one example of how the language conveys the vision that
cannot be otherwise conveyed: when the earth beneath our
feet is first mentioned near the end of section 2, it is "dust,"
in sharp contrast with "life" and "spirit"—as it is in Genesis
2:7, when the Lord formed man from "the dust of the
ground, and breathed into his nostrils the breath of life; and
man became a living soul"; and as it is also in Genesis 3:19:
"for dust thou art, and unto dust shalt thou return." Then, in
the last line of this section, the "dust" becomes "sand," which
is still negative and may suggest a desert hostile to life but
does not carry the biblical suggestion of the antithesis of
"soul" the way "dust" does. When the same earth is referred
to three times in the poem's last section, it is first "dirt,"
which is more negative than positive ("dirty"), then "ground,"
which is positive in both literal and metaphoric senses (your
"feet on the ground," "the ground of being"), and finally
"soil," the most positive of all, since it is what nourishes the
life on this planet. The objective substance referred to has not
changed, but the way it is "seen" has changed from negative

to positive, permitting the last lines to convey not a merely
poetic fancy but an earned feeling:

> And I walked, I walked through the light air;
> I moved with the morning.

The volume ends, a little less memorably perhaps, with
"The Shape of the Fire," which follows the same movement
from despairing loss of relation and of true vision ("Where's
the eye? / The eye's in the sty. . . . An eye comes out of the
wave") to recovery of the ability to see and thus

> To know that light falls and fills, often without our knowing,
> As an opaque vase fills to the brim from a quick pouring,
> Fills and trembles at the edge yet does not flow over,
> Still holding and feeding the stem of the contained flower.

★   ★   ★

The four volumes Roethke published between *The Lost Son*
and *The Far Field* contain some of his finest poems but not
many that treat the problematics of vision in the way the
ending of "The Lost Son" and "A Field of Light" do. Not
until his "North American Sequence" in the final volume
would Roethke explore farther along the path first marked
out by Whitman.

Still, many of the poems in the intermediate volumes
remind us of "Cuttings" and "A Field of Light," even when
they take their cue from different impulses and develop in
different directions. "Praise to the End," for instance, begins
and ends this way:

> It's dark in this wood, soft mocker.
> . . . .
> The dark showed me a face.
> My ghosts are all gay.
> The light becomes me.

Between these opening and closing lines, though, the power of the poem seems to spring from the way it takes enormous risks in its use of normally private experience as it moves from narcissism to relationship. Again, isolated lines in "I Cry, Love! Love!" may remind us of Emerson, Whitman, or even E. E. Cummings—"Hello, thingy spirit," "I proclaim once more a condition of joy," "Behold, in the lout's eye, / Love," for instance—but only the final section of the poem fits the visionary paradigm by discovering once again in perceptual experience reason to believe that "we never enter / Alone."

Even more clearly, "Four for Sir John Davies"—surely one of Roethke's most memorable poems—does not develop in the visionary way either formally or thematically despite its ambiguous last line, "The word outleaps the world, and light is all," in which both "word" and "light" have metaphoric overtones and carry religious suggestions. Rather, as a series of meditative religious lyrics, the poem as a whole prepares us for the visionary poems in *The Far Field* by suggesting the movement beyond the early "nature mysticism" toward the greater kinship with historic Christianity that became fully apparent in the posthumous volume and gave that work its special character.

"The Vigil," for instance, presents the difficulties facing the spiritual son of Emerson and Thoreau who wants to believe that "the flesh can make the spirit visible." He finds himself, as he yearns for a vision of harmony comparable to Dante's, in a "dark world where Gods have lost their way" and decides that "the visible obscures. But who knows when?" Today it seems that the dance is "slowing in the mind of man / That made him think the universe could hum," though perhaps lovers can "live by longing and endure: / Summon a vision and declare it pure":

> Rapt, we leaned forth with what we could not see.
> We danced to shining, mocked before the black
> And shapeless night that made no answer back.

As the "shining" in these lines is more willed than perceived, so "A Walk in Late Summer" seems to assert rather
than to perceive trancendence. "A gull rides on the ripples of
a dream," but can dreams be trusted? Is the gull really there,
reflecting an order in the world, not just in the poem? "God's
in that stone, or I am not a man!" We must believe that

> Body and soul transcend appearances
> Before the caving-in of all that is;
> I'm dying piecemeal, fervent in decay;
> My moments linger—that's eternity.

Perhaps only "the eye of faith" can see that the "late
rose" that "ravages the casual eye" is really "a blaze of being
on a central stem." As the light fades and the poem draws to
its conclusion, religious echoes of past belief become more
frequent, as in the archaism of "tree" for "cross":

> A tree arises on a central plain—
> It is no trick of change or chance of light.
> A tree all out of shape from wind and rain,
> A tree thinned by the wind obscures my sight.
> The long day dies; I walked the woods alone;
> Beyond the ridge two wood thrush sing as one.
> Being delights in being, and in time.
> The evening wraps me, steady as a flame.

"The Dying Man," dedicated to Yeats and alluding to
"Sailing to Byzantium," both continues the consideration of
the difficulty of achieving true vision—"Though it reject dry
borders of the seen, / What sensual eye can keep an image

pure, / Leaning across a sill to greet the dawn?"—and defines Roethke's sense of his difference from the older visionary poet who had meant, and still meant, so much to him. Yeats's artificial birds, though created by the most skilled gold-smiths so perfectly as to excel the beauty of nature, could not satisfy a poet unwilling to settle for the poetic or imagined "artifice of eternity" that Yeats's poem had seen as the poet's ultimate gift to us:

> I've the lark's word for it, who sings alone:
> What's seen recedes; Forever's what we know!—
> Eternity defined, and strewn with straw,
> The fury of the slug beneath the stone.
> The vision moves, and yet remains the same.
> In heaven's praise, I dread the thing I am.

Roethke's "singing masters" in his final volume would be poets who had not just imagined or created order and har-mony but, as Roethke believed, discovered it—with the aid of the imagination, considered as noetic, to be sure, but with-out cutting the imagination's ties to the "real":

> The edges of the summit still appall
> When we brood on the dead or the beloved;
> Nor can imagination do it all
> In this last place of light: he dares to live
> Who stops being a bird, yet beats his wings
> Against the immense immeasurable emptiness of
>   things.

★　★　★

But of course once we realize that imagination and belief are unavoidably involved in the movement from the seen to the known, doubt begins. Are we seeing with the mind's eye what we want to see, or what our culture has prepared us to

see? Does the subjective element in visual perception make
everything uncertain? We are not likely to doubt the reality
of a blow, of the nauseous smell, or of the acrid taste, but we
may well doubt whether the object that appears to be more
distant really is so, or whether the heavens reveal the glory
of God or merely a universe of chance. A visionary poem
may help us to see what is missed by "the casual eye," but
neither a visionary poem nor even a visionary experience can
ever "prove" anything.

Could the possibility of doubt be a prerequisite of the
visionary, whether experience or poem? Only the successful
Imagist poem seems impossible to doubt—unless we go outside the poem to analyze the cultural, philosophic, and perceptual assumptions that underlie it but are barriers, not aids,
to a sympathetic reading of it as an aesthetic object. Even the
mystic today, aware of Freud, may doubt his own mystical
experiences. Were the visions and voices, or even the
"oceanic feeling" of Union, projected or perceived? He may
feel the unarguable certainty described by William James, but
what if in certain moods he is not satisfied with feeling and
wants to know?

We should not be surprised then to find the doubt, darkness, and self-distrust in which so many of the late poems
begin deeper and more concretely realized than at any time
since "The Lost Son," while at the same time the affirmations
of transcendence with which they generally end are at once
more assured and farther removed from the relative "certain-
ties" of the visually perceptible. It should come as no surprise
either that in "Once More, the Round," with which the final
sequence concludes, the controlling image should come not
from nature but from culture, and that the poet's dancing
partner should be William Blake. Roethke wrote his greatest

visionary poems in "North American Sequence," in the tradition initiated by Whitman, then ended his career in "Sequence, Sometimes Metaphysical" as Whitman had his, by turning from the seen to the unseen. "Incarnational" perhaps more aptly describes many of the late poems than "visionary." This was where "the long journey out of the self" finally brought him.

Still, Roethke's very finest work seems to me to be found not in the latest poems but in the poems I have called visionary. "Meditation at Oyster River" never lets the reader forget either part of its title. The meditation is not free-floating but tied to the ongoing life of Oyster River, the "setting" as we might call it if that word did not tend to suggest a merely inert place where something is done or happens or "takes place." But the "setting" in the poem is no mere location, "the scene of the action," but is in effect one of the actors, the other being the poet who perceives and responds. The result is a poem to which our traditional labels do not seem to apply.

Although, for instance, the poem could hardly be further removed from the Imagist ideal of objective description, it is not in any traditional sense a Symbolist poem either. It seems to move not by the free association of the multiple suggestions of words, as it might if Hart Crane had written it, but in response to "things," as if Roethke were remembering Whitman's idea in "Song of the Rolling Earth" that "the substantial words are in the ground and the sea." And in another way, too, the poem may remind us of Whitman: I know of no other poem that comes so close to translating into the language and sensibility of our century the situation and thematic development of "Out of the cradle, Endlessly Rocking," even to the role of the sea, which both drowns and rocks, and the birds, which the speaker in the later poem finds "graceful . . . before danger," as he would like to learn to be.

But despite their similarities, even to the phrases "rocking the cradle" and "in the cradle" in the endings of the two poems, there seems no reason to think of Whitman's poem as a conscious model for Roethke's. Perhaps the greatest difference between them is the closer attention the later speaker must pay to the world that surrounds and includes him, which is part of him as he is part of it, so that its "meaning," if any, can be discovered only by letting it suggest its own word. This speaker's attentiveness at the edge of the sea seems less active and purposive than Whitman's "cautiously peering, absorbing, translating" the meaning of the song of the bird. "Peering" and "translating" seem unneeded here.

In the estuary called Oyster River, distinctions lose their sharp edges as river and sea blend, land and sea alter their outlines, and the light fails. The incoming tide threatens to engulf the speaker until he moves "to a rock higher up the cliff-side." The "elephant-colored rocks" and the "rows of dead clam shells" of the opening lines of the first section are temporal equivalents of the rising of the water as it submerges the land, so that, "with no sound from the bay," there seems no need to translate the archetypal images.

Early in the poem, the speaker sees a "fish raven . . . on its perch (a dead tree in the rivermouth), / Its wings catching a last glint of the reflected sunlight." That ravens are black gets no comment, and its silence here prompts no translation comparable to Poe's "Nevermore," but its presence above the "blue-black" water of the approaching sea prepares us for the opening lines of the next section, "The self persists like a dying star, / In sleep, afraid. Death's face rises afresh." Yet at the same time the light reflected on its wing anticipates in a minor key the full moonlight in which the poem ends, a reflected light prompting reflection:

> In the first of the moon,
> All's a scattering,
> A shining.

Neither the raven nor the sandpiper in the final section ("intrepid shorebirds— / How graceful the small before danger") seems a symbol, like Eliot's kingfisher in "Burnt Norton," which can be translated "fisher-king," or Christ, bringing light to a dark world, or like Poe's raven. What is seen and heard at Oyster River becomes the substance of the meditation.

So too with "Journey to the Interior," which I might choose as Roethke's greatest visionary poem if I had to choose just one. The geographic journey and the metaphoric journey of self-discovery and self-transcendence are never separated—"the road was part of me"—so that once again there seems to be no need to explain how something symbolizes something else. When the recalled journey is over and the meditative interpretation of it comes in the last section, we are asked to accept no great claim:

> I have heard, in a drip of leaves,
> A slight song,
> After the midnight cries.

And the vision that has been sufficiently achieved to enable the speaker to say that he has "seen" and "known the heart of the sun,— / In the dark and light of a dry place" is expressed in the "as if" form of the simile that seems fully earned by the time we read it in the opening of the final lines: "As a blind man, lifting a curtain, knows it is morning, / I know this change."

Three features of the poem seem to me largely responsible for its power as a visionary poem: the detailed "realism" of the remembered physical journey, the archetypal extensions of the dominant physical images that prepare us for the vision expressed in the poem's last section, and the unemphatic presence of several biblical echoes.

The concreteness is nothing new in Roethke's poems, but here it is, if anything, more detailed and convincingly personal than ever, as just two passages should sufficiently illustrate. First, the beginning of the journey:

> In the long journey out of the self,
> There are many detours, washed-out interrupted raw places
> Where the shale slides dangerously
> And the back wheels hang almost over the edge
> At the sudden veering, the moment of turning.
> Better to hug close, wary of rubble and falling stones.
> The arroyo cracking the road, the wind-bitten buttes, the
>   canyons,
> Creeks swollen in midsummer from the flash-flood roaring
>   into the narrow valley.
> ....
> I remember how it was to drive in gravel,
> Watching for dangerous down-hill places, where the wheels
>   whined beyond eighty—
> When you hit the deep pit at the bottom of the swale,
> The trick was to throw the car sideways and charge over the
>   hill, full of the throttle.

In the course of the journey, the driver passes through towns deep in the interior,

> Their wooden stores of silvery pine and weather-beaten
>   red courthouses,

An old bridge below with a buckled iron railing,
    broken by some idiot plunger;
Underneath, the sluggish water running between
    weeds, broken wheels, tires, stones.
And all flows past—
The cemetery with two scrubby trees in the middle of
    the prairie,
The dead snakes and muskrats, the turtles gasping in
    the rubble,
The spikey purple bushes in the winding dry creek
    bed—
The floating hawks, the jackrabbits, the grazing cattle—

Like the "interior" of the title, which is literal where
applied to the continent but metaphoric where applied to the
self, the archetypal suggestions of *journey*, *road*, *water*, *light*,
and *dark*, which are central in the poem from beginning to
end, would seem to need no explications, after all that the
depth-psychologists, the anthropologists, and the historians
of comparative religion have done with them—unless it were
simply to say that their presence in the poem does not make
it seem in the least "mythy." The verisimilitude makes all the
difference. The things we encounter in the poem seem real
things in a physical world, not illustrations of any system of
thought.

As for the biblical echoes, there are two as I see it, with
the first preparing us for the second but going by so casually
that it may remain unnoticed. The narrowness of the road
described early in the poem is twice mentioned explicitly and
vividly put before us implicitly as perhaps the chief difficulty
of the hazardous journey, and we remember that Jesus is
quoted in Matthew 7:14 as warning of the same difficulty:
"Because strait [that is, narrow] is the gate, and narrow is the
way, which leadeth unto life, and few there be that find it."

The second echo is more emphatic but tied not to any particular biblical passage but to both the Old and New Testaments, from Genesis to Paul's letters, as a glance at a biblical concordance with its columns devoted to "wrath" and "blessing" will quickly show. The last two lines of the poem then do not depend upon but gain further overtones of meaning from the Bible: "The spirit of wrath becomes the spirit of blessing, / And the dead begin from their dark to sing in my sleep." The external journey is interpreted in dream in these final lines but not forgotten or betrayed. So concretely grounded a poetic visionary affirmation can be taken seriously.

★   ★   ★

Still, dreams end and we wake to more dark times and new uncertainties. The ambiguities of the visible reappear and refuse to be believed or dreamed away. Although in a dark time the visionary eye may begin to see, adjusting itself to the darkness as the literal eye does, still "the edge" is what we have and "the purity of pure despair" remains balanced against the hope that we have seen truly when we perceived "a steady stream of correspondences." "In a Dark Time," the opening lyric in Roethke's final "Sequence, Sometimes Metaphysical," achieves the Transcendental affirmation in its final lines—"The mind enters itself, and God the Mind, / And one is One, free in the tearing wind"—not so much by learning to see the implicit meaning of the world outside the self as by coming to terms with the self, in effect by a "journey" through the personal, moral, and psychological "interior." Only "the death of the self in a long tearless night" can now make it seem that "all natural shapes [are] blazing unnatural light."

"*Unnatural* light": like Whitman before him, Roethke found at last as he lived with the premonition of the early death that came to him that though "vision" can forerun "the identities of the spiritual world," still, what is perceived even by the poet's eye remains "removed from any proof but its own." If so, "what shakes the eye but the invisible?"

No wonder then that the greatest visionary poet of our century, and the last one—till now at least—able to make meaningful and moving use of God-language, should have returned to a "metaphysical" way of writing in the last poems he worked on before his death. Although he still hoped to "teach my eyes to hear, my ears to see," so that "the deep eye" could see "the shimmer on the stone," there was little time left. Knowing that "Eternity's not easily come by," he could wonder, "Was I too glib about eternal things?" Memory could remind him, as it had Whitman before him, that once "I became all that I looked upon," but now that was not enough and he was moved to prayer:

> Lord, hear me out, and hear me out this day:
> From me to Thee's a long and terrible way.
> . . . .
> Sweet Christ, rejoice in my infirmity:
> . . . .
> My soul is still my soul, and still the Son,
> And knowing this, I am not yet undone.

Acutely aware now that the dancing figure he had often seemed to see in the wind may have been not "objectively" *there* but merely a "shape called up" by the mind, he continued his often-repeated "long journey out of the self" by relying on senses less easy to question than vision. Images of movement reminiscent of the kinesthic imagery in the early

"Night Journey" dominate the final poems of the sequence. "Running," "rising," and "falling" are the guiding sensations in "The Decision," as the muscular harmonies induced by dancing are central in "The Restored."

As to how much we may trust poetic vision, "let others probe the mystery if they can," we read in "The Right Thing," which concludes in a way reminiscent of another earlier poem, "The Waking": "The right thing happens to the happy man." Even though the eye, so easily influenced by the will, may not so much disclose as alter the seen, so that the visible leaves the "Unknown" what it has always been, still the "identity" that Whitman had once thought "real vision" could discern could be affirmed and celebrated in the ordered motion of the dance. "Once More, the Round" brings Roethke's poetic career to its natural, and triumphant, conclusion:

> What's greater, Pebble or Pond?
> What can be known? The Unknown.
> My true self runs toward a Hill
> More! O More! visible.
>
> Now I adore my life
> With the Bird, the abiding Leaf,
> With the Fish, the questing Snail,
> And the Eye altering all;
> And I dance with William Blake
> For love, for Love's sake;
>
> And everything comes to One,
> As we dance on, dance on, dance on.

★   ★   ★

Note: Roethke and Mysticism   Although *The Far Field* has been viewed both as a decline into religious maundering and

as the triumphant achievement of a modern mystic, depending on the bias of the reviewer, not even Ralph Mills has
noted how closely the lyrics in "North American Sequence"
parallel the "stages" of the Western, especially Christian,
mystical experience as described by Evelyn Underhill.
Whether consciously intended or not—though Roethke had
read and pondered Underhill's book by this time—the parallels are close enough to prepare us for the shift of attention
announced in "The Decision" in the poet's final "Sequence,
Sometimes Metaphysical":

1

> What shakes the eye but the invisible?
> Running from God's the longest race of all.
> A bird kept haunting me when I was young—
> The phoebe's slow retreating from its song,
> Nor could I put that sound out of my mind,
> The sleepy sound of leaves in a light wind.

2

> Rising or falling's all one discipline!
> The line of my horizon's growing thin!
> Which is the way? I cry to the dread black,
> The shifting shade, the cinders at my back.
> Which is the way? I ask, and turn to go,
> As a man turns to face on-coming snow.

It requires no forcing to read the lyrics in "North American Sequence" as expressions of Underhill's five stages of the
mystical experience, in the order in which she lists them,
without any "inversion" like that which James Miller found
necessary when he applied the scheme to "Song of Myself."
"The Longing," which opens the sequence, describes a spiri-

tual "awakening": "On things asleep no balm," the first line declares, while the final lines announce Roethke's intention to be an explorer of the "invisible" spiritual realities as, drawing on Eliot's ending of "Little Gidding," he writes

> Old men should be explorers?
> I'll be an Indian.
> Ogalala?
> Iroquois.

He will explore in a native way, "without benefit of clergy," as he wrote in his Notebook, as one already well acquainted with the land, but more like the settled, "civilized" Iroquois than like the roving, warlike Ogalala band of Sioux hunters. No Anglo-Catholicism, or making do with small epiphanies in the rose garden, for him. Even though, with Eliot, he longs for "the imperishable quiet at the heart of form," he wishes not to stop "delighting in the redolent disorder of this mortal life."

To cut what could easily become a long story short, "Meditation at Oyster River" may be read as a kind of secular baptism, or "Purification" by water, as the speaker first dabbles his toes in the incoming tide, then finally is able to declare that "water's my will, and my way." Similarly, "Journey to the Interior" ends with an "Illumination" that no longer depends on visual perception:

> As a blind man, lifting a curtain, knows it is morning,
> I know this change:
> On one side of silence there is no smile;
> But when I breathe with the birds,
> The spirit of wrath becomes the spirit of blessing,
> And the dead begin from their dark to sing in my sleep.

"The Long Waters" tests the illumination by a return to

"the charred edge of the sea" where fire has blackened the land and "the fresh and salt waters meet," with the speaker finding, again like Whitman in "Faces," that he has help in facing the sea, that he is not alone:

> I see in the advancing and retreating waters
> The shape that came from my sleep, weeping:
> The eternal one, the child, the swaying vine branch,
> The numinous ring around the opening flower,
> The friend that runs before me on the windy headlands,
> Neither voice nor vision.
> I, who came back from the depths laughing too loudly,
> Become another thing;
> My eyes extend beyond the farthest bloom of the waves;
> I lose and find myself in the long water;
> I am gathered together once more;
> I embrace the world.

A vision of "the eternal one, the child," like the face of "the Master" in Whitman's poem, has made it possible for him to "embrace the world" even as he rejects "the world of the dog" and encounters "unsinging fields where no lungs breathe." "The Far Field" begins in the mystics' "Dark Night of the Soul" with a memory of a dreamlike journey to the end of the road where "the headlights darken," and ends with an anticipation of approaching death—"An old man with his feet before the fire, / In robes of green, in garments of adieu."

"The Rose" develops what Underhill and others have described as the mystical experience of "Union"—"I sway outside myself / Into the darkening currents"—with a final allusion to "Little Gidding" as the poet reaffirms his choice of "this place, where sea and fresh water meet," over Eliot's chapel, and finds himself at last outside himself, "beyond becoming and perishing," as he sways "out on the wildest wave alive, / And yet was still":

> And in this rose, this rose in the sea-wind,
> Rooted in stone, keeping the whole of light,
> Gathering to itself sound and silence—
> Mine and the sea-wind's.

To me, the concluding affirmation of "The Rose" seems a little forced, as though the poet's reading of Underhill and his discontent with Eliot's minor rose garden epiphanies had led him to affirm as achieved what was still only wished for. His question in the later sequence, "Was I too glib about eternal things?" may, for some readers, seem to apply to "The Rose," in which he seems to forget, or transcend too easily, his lifelong ambivalent reaction to his father:

> What need for heaven, then,
> With that man and those roses?

But perhaps another question asked in the later sequence throws some light on what strikes me as the willed aspect of the final affirmations in this poem: "How can I dream except beyond this life?"

CHAPTER VI

A. R. Ammons

Ezra "Perishing for Deity"

Both Ammons' *Selected Poems* (1968) and his misnamed *Collected Poems* (1972) open with "So I Said I Am Ezra," a poem from his first volume announcing his preoccupation and his conception of his role as a poet. The Ezra who serves as mock-serious model in the poem, often referred to as a "minor prophet," is classified in the Old Testament as one of the Chroniclers and is described as "Ezra the priest, the scribe, even a scribe of the words of the commandments of the Lord" (Ezra 7:11), or, in the language of the Jerusalem Bible, "a scribe versed in the Law of Moses, which had been given by Yahweh," who had "devoted himself to the study of the Law of Yahweh" (Ezra 7:6, 10). In similar fashion, Robert Frost had announced himself in the later editions of his *Collected Poems* with "The Pasture" ("I'm going out to clean the pasture spring"). The difference is that Frost took his role seriously, whereas Ammons is laughing at himself in "So I Said I Am Ezra."

The original Ezra is remembered in connection with the rebuilding of the Temple after the Babylonian Exile, and the laws he studied were thought to have been Revealed to Moses on the mountain. Writing today, he would presumably know that his proper study should be the laws of nature, revealed not to Moses but to scientists, not on the mountain but in the laboratory, and not by Yahweh but by "the great vacuity" that had replaced Him and in which "all at last must be lost," including devout scribes like himself. He would know this especially if he had majored in biology, worked in a laboratory, and been influenced by his reading in Eastern religious literature, with its conception of the ultimate reality as "Nothing." An Ezra today, knowing that vacuums do not carry sound, would expect no answer when

> Turning to the sea I said
> I am Ezra

> but there were no echoes from the waves
> The words were swallowed up
> in the voice of the surf[1]

The linking of poet and prophet is of course an idea with as long a history as the linking of poet and artisan or maker, but why Ezra? Why not one of the major prophets? For several reasons, as I see it. The idea of poet as prophet arouses amused smiles today, so that a poet who half-believes he has a prophetic message will protect himself by choosing to identify with a "minor," widely forgotten, "prophet" who is chiefly distinguished not for any prophetic utterances but for the fact that, in a time when few could read and write, he was a scribe and chronicler. And not only a chronicler of history but especially prepared for his task by devotion to study of the laws of the Almighty. Today, thinking of Isaiah, Ezekiel, or Jeremiah, we expect a prophet to hear voices, experience visions, or speak as a moral critic of his people; Ezra we would call a priestly scholar and perhaps a devout "intellectual." Ammons chose well when, with self-directed irony, he presented himself in the role of a modern Ezra. When he discarded the role in *Snow Poems*, his poetry became much less interesting. With nothing more to say to us, for the time being, about the laws of the microscopic and macroscopic physical and temporal world in relation to the ultimate vacuity that had replaced the first Ezra's Yahweh, his poetry became self-pitying, self-indulgent, and boring.

★   ★   ★

In the early poems, the "seen" and the "unseen" are in tension. In them, "a poem is a walk" taken with all our senses

---

1   A. R. Ammons, *Collected Poems, 1951–1971* (New York, 1972), 1. Unless otherwise noted, subsequent quotations from Ammons' verse are from this edition.

alert to miss nothing that can be seen or guessed or foreseen. Facticity is dominant, but transcendence, muted in possibility, seems always just over the horizon, hoped for rather than precisely known, but hoped for with eyes open and mind alert. Such cautious hope would be very different from the merely wishful "imagining" of earlier, less realistic "visionaries." In "Corsons Inlet" it bears no resemblance to the self-delusion pictured in another early poem, "Mountain Liar":

> The mountains said they were
> tired of lying down
> and wanted to know what
> I could do about
> getting them off the ground
>
> Well close your eyes I said
> and I'll see if I can
> by seeing into your nature
> tell where you've been wronged
> What do you think you want to do
> They said Oh fly
>
> My hands are old
> and crippled keep no lyre
> but if that is your true desire
> and conforms roughly
> with your nature I said
> I don't see why
> we shouldn't try
> to see something along that line
>
> Hurry they said and snapped shut
> with rocky sounds their eyes
> I closed mine and sure enough
> the whole range flew
> gliding on interstellar ice

> They shrieked with joy and peeked
>> as if to see below
> but saw me as before there
>> foolish without my lyre
> We haven't budged they said
>> You wood

The poet in this poem has achieved his "vision" by closing his eyes and persuading the mountains to close theirs: flight achieved only in fantasy is impossible to maintain when we open our eyes to the facts. The poet wants nothing to do with "make-believe."

But the distinction between truly seeing and merely "imagining" need not be so clear. In a good many of the most memorable early poems, the distinction is in fact far from clear. Two poems, "Raft" and "Corsons Inlet," may serve to illustrate the tension between facticity and meaningful order that energizes the best early work. That the source of the tension is indeed the hard-to-draw distinction between the "seens" and the "unseen" or "implicit" is made clear in the opening lines of another poem of the same period, "Turning a Moment to Say So Long":

> Turning a moment to say so long
>> to the spoken
>> and seen
>> I stepped into
> the implicit pausing sometimes
> on the way to listen to unsaid things
> At a boundary of mind
>> Oh I said brushing up
>> against the unseen
>> and whirling on my heel
>> said
> I have overheard too much. . . .

"Raft," from Ammons' second early volume, *Expressions of Sea Level*, describes an imagined venture of the spirit into the unknown with only the playful tone of the poem to protect the poet from the charge of being a "romantic visionary." The comic personification of the opening stanza, in which we hear the voice of a child calling to the wind to be his playmate, "communing" with nature as his friend, tells us how to read this ultimately serious poem about the poet's "inspiration" and where it takes him:

> I called the wind and it
> went over with me
> to the bluff
> that keeps the sea-bay
> and we stayed around for a while
> trying to think
> what to do:

Before he begins his play with the wind (*spiritus*: wind, breath; inspiration and expiration; "Holy Spirit"), the child pauses to look around: "I took some time to watch / the tall reeds. . . . I could not think but / vanished into the beauty / of any thing I saw / and loved." Finally remembering what he had come to do, the child "wove a disc of reeds, / a round raft," and found himself carried by the outgoing tide "into the open sea." There, beyond sight of land, "tide free and without direction," having drifted all night, he "knelt in the center" of his round raft that could no longer be poled in any chosen direction and watched "for where the / sun would break" that he might at least know in which direction he was facing as his raft turned. He was "not certain" he "wanted to go east" but

> it seemed wise
> to let

the currents be
whatever they would be,
allowing possibility
to chance
where choice
could not impose itself:

I knelt turning that way
a long time,
glad I had brought my great
round hat
for the sun got hot:

The poem ends as the sun is setting again "and the wind came / in an afternoon way / rushing before dark to catch me." The movement has been a voluntary one into the unseen and unknown, playfully so that the reader will not confuse the literal and the metaphoric, but without any suggestion of final hopelessness. "Raft" is as romantic a poem as Ammons has ever published. His later development would be away from the guarded but still real confidence in inspiration and away from the willingness to do without willed control implied in this poem, in which the building of the raft that will carry him to the open sea is "what I came to do."

"Corsons Inlet" is an equally hopeful visionary poem in an even less guarded way. It can afford to be less guarded because it is not dependent, as "Raft" is, on traditional—and archetypal—images like land, sea, and wind. Instead, after the casual, conversational opening lines, "I went for a walk over the dunes again this morning / to the sea," the movement of the poem seems fully directed by what the walker perceives during the walk, with the finite details of the seen prompting frequent passages of reflection on the unseen. In

the subdued light of a "continuous overcast" now, the
speaker finds the walk "liberating," so that he feels

>   released from forms,
>   from the perpendiculars,
>   straight lines, blocks, boxes, binds
>   of thought
>   into the hues, shadings, rises, flowing bends and blends
>   of sight:

With no desire this time to move into the open sea out
of sight of land, where he knows he would discover that
"Overall is beyond me," he finds himself reflecting that "in
nature there are few sharp lines," reminding himself that he
has "reached no conclusions, . . . erected no boundaries,"
and is "willing to go along, to accept / the becoming"—
though "becoming," with its colloquial rather than its philosophic meaning, suggests the first word of the next line,
"thought." (The speaker is willing to limit his thinking to
Becoming, avoiding the problem of Being; such thought
strikes him as more "becoming.") What can be perceived is
enough: he will have "no humbling of reality to precept."
Watching a flight of tree swallows, he sees

>   a congregation
>   rich with entropy: nevertheless, separable, noticeable
>   as one event,
>   not chaos: preparations for
>   flight from winter,
>   cheet, cheet, cheet, cheet, wings rifling the green
>   clumps,
>   beaks
>   at the bayberries
>   a perception full of wind, flight, curve,
>   sound:

> the possibility of rule as the sum of rulelessness:
> the "field" of action
> with moving, incalculable center:

Although he says he has "reached no conclusions," what he has experienced during the walk has seemed to offer support for some ideas about the nature of becoming, if not about Being, the "Overall" that is beyond him; for instance, and centrally, the realization that, for all life, "risk is full: every living thing in / siege: the demand is life, to keep life." He has seen the *evidence* of this. From the beginning, the poem has moved from the empirical to the conceptual, so that the reader is prepared to accept the way "see" and "vision" in the final lines have lost all literal meaning and become metaphors for *understand* or *interpret* and even for provisional *belief:*

> I see narrow orders, limited tightness, but will
> not run to that easy victory:
>   still around the looser, wider forces work:
>   I will try
>   to fasten into order enlarging grasps of disorder,
>   widening
> scope, but enjoying the freedom that
> Scope eludes my grasp, that there is no finality of vision,
> that I have perceived nothing completely,
>   that tomorrow a new walk is a new walk.

Despite its much-emphasized skepticism, "Corsons Inlet" still finds Ammons writing as a kind of modern Ezra for whom the "laws" he seeks to understand were not written on tablets or to be found in scholarly commentaries but are to be inferred from the natural world. (Emerson: Nature is our Scripture.) Although the poem never speaks of "correspon-

dences" and makes no overt attempt to intuit the nature of
the "Overall," its toned-down neo-Transcendentalism is apparent. Emerson, too, in "The Bohemian Hymn" had declared what he usually preferred to call the Oversoul indefinable by language or learning. In some of his later work,
Ammons abandoned the role of Ezra, but in "Corsons Inlet"
it has not yet been dropped or made the subject of a joke, and
he has seldom written better.

★ ★ ★

Reading through the later verse before *Snow Poems*, we find
the physical world of the senses less and less concretely presented in verse that still abstractly insists on its importance.
As the poems become more "intellectual," the world of thought
or "reason" takes its place as that which nourishes the imagination sufficiently to become the subject of poems. This
modern Ezra had of course believed all along that "the eternal
will not lie / down on any temporal hill," as Emerson had
before him, but in the later poems the balance between perception and mind that still seems preserved even in "Mechanism"—where we find "mind / or perception rising into or-
ders of courtship"—is upset. Mind becomes the dominant
partner, until finally there are no more round rafts built and
hopefully embarked on and, it would appear, no more ex-
ploratory walks taken beyond the bounds of the suburban
yard. Nature is thought about a good deal by the poet in his
study. But with nature become an abstraction and the poet
still distrusting the "binds of thought," the question finally
becomes what to write about.

But before that happened, Ammons wrote a good many
very impressive poems, poems that—though they seem only
marginally related to the visionary mode and mood—still
indulge in enough tentative sallies beyond the mundane to
leave room for feelings of wonder. Two of the best of such

poems intermediate between the youthful spirit of "Raft" and the tired resignation of *Snow Poems* seem to me *Tape for the Turn of the Year* and *Sphere*.

Tape is an antipoetic, "free form," diarylike poem typed on a roll of adding-machine tape, as the poet tells us, to keep the lines short, and so, as we may guess, to throw the emphasis on discrete words and specific perceptions, difficult to achieve in the classic poetic forms. The poem may well strike us at first as a kind of poetic joke directed against poetry itself, the visionary, and particularly the visionary poetry of the past, with its power of luring us into suspending our disbelief. In effect, the poet invites the reader into his study to observe the poet at work: participating in the process this way should cure him of any delusion he may still harbor that the poet is some sort of prophet:

> today I
> decided to write
> a long
>> thin
>> poem
>
>> employing certain
> classical considerations:
>>> this
> part is called the pro-
> logue: it has to do with
>> the business of
>> getting started:[2]

The "long thin poem" that follows for 205 pages ("poem must be now / close to 40 feet long") is divided into thirty-three sections headed by the dates on which the poet's ran-

---

2 *Tape for the Turn of the Year* (Ithaca, N.Y., 1965), 1. All subsequent quotations from this work are taken from this edition.

dom thoughts were recorded, beginning December 6 and
ending, to the poet's expressed relief, when the roll of tape
ran out on January 10. Any reader who still confuses Archie
with Ezra is explicitly warned that what he is reading is just
a poem the poet has made, not to be confused with prophetic
vision of any sort, by however minor a prophet:

> if it ain't one fantasy
> it's anothern: where
> > are you, reality?
> > come out of there:
>
> ....
>
> all this is just coming
> out of my head:
> the factory of fantasies:
> some beautiful, some
> terrifying,
> some this, some that—but
> all, paper & thin air!

The reader who, thus warned of what not to expect, continues to the end, will be thanked for his persistence:

> the roll has lifted
> from the floor &
> our journey is done:
> thank you
> for coming: thank
> you for coming along:

   In a sense, then, the poem is about the nature of poetry,
about how poetry is written, and about how the poet is a
craftsman like any other, subject to interruptions, unable, or
unwilling, to work some days, glad to have the job over
when the tape runs out. But this aspect of the poem, which

reminds us of Williams' Hartpence story—"That, Madam, is paint"—seems ultimately only cautionary. The age-old concerns of the visionary and prophetic are not really given up after all: again and again they creep in despite all the implicit and explicit warnings against being taken in by fantasies posing as veritable visions.

For along with the confessions and the jokes, we are given serious reasons why the poem takes the form it does, and the reasons have to do with the poet's view of the relations of vision, language, and visionary poetry. Thus we read that traditional poetic forms, including the long line, are avoided to protect the integrity of specific perceptions from the shaping, altering power of mind:

> an object,
> exactly perceived
> & described is
> when entered in the
>   tapestry
> somewhat compromised:
> part strength flows
> from it
> to its
> compositional environment:

The poet's job is to try to make language convey the seen as immediately seen, prior to interpretation. That is why, originally, he says,

> I had
> decided to
> give up all
> but details.

So he writes the poem as he does because the "facts are that

way": "I care about the statement / of fact." Emerson's
motto, "Look to the fact for the form," is rephrased again
and again here. If the poet can remember to do this, and if
his skill with words is great enough, his vision, in both the
literal and the metaphoric senses, will come to seem to be
ours, his truth our truth:

>   . . . the
>   truths poetry creates
>   die with
>   their language:
>   stir any old
>   language up,
>   feel the fire in it &
>   its truths come true
>   again:
>   the resource, the
>   creation, and the end of
>   poetry is
>   language:
>   ....
>
>   poetry is art & is
>   artificial: but it
>   realizes reality's
>   potentials:

But what are reality's potentials? What "truths" would
Ammons as a poet in an age of unbelief have us accept as our
own? What, in short, apart from poetry itself, is the poem
"about"? We are told in the lines written on, or at least as-
signed to, the last day of the year that "poetry has / one subject, impermanence, / which it presents / with as much permanence as / possible," but though we are never allowed to

forget the passage of time for long, the poet's thoughts turn very often to permanence, or at least to that which is more lasting than we are. From these thoughts of the poet, presented as in effect self-indulgences, we can isolate three recurring themes that it is possible to say the poem is "about."

The first is nature, of which of course we are a part. Although it is almost wholly absent from the poem's imagery, this is the reality we must study to learn its full potential. How can the poet learn to see it better, see it more truly?

> I beg that my eyes that are
> open
> be opened, that the
>   drives, motions,
> intellections, symbologies,
> myths—lift,
>   expose me
> to direct
> sight: seeing, I
> color, alter, hide, accent:
> but what is there, naked
>   & nonhuman?

As he watches a snowfall through his study window, the poet realizes that he can "react with / restlessness and quiet / terror, or with / fascination & / delight: I choose the / side of possibility." "Ecology," he tells us, is the word to tag him with. He's a "celebrant" of nature, as the way he chooses to use his last remaining bit of tape suggests:

> the sun's bright:
> the wind rocks the
> naked trees:
> so long.

Secondly, the skepticism that runs through the poem, directed against any uncritical rationalism ("mind") more often than against the outmoded religious beliefs that once "haunted" us, may be turned around and seen in the insistence on the permanence of mystery. Although we must be careful not to see too subjectively, we must be equally careful to avoid supposing that we have banished, or soon will, mystery, for if that should happen, we would be imprisoned:

> release us from mental
> prisons into the actual
>   fact, the mere
>   occurrence—the touched,
> tasted, heard, seen:
>   in the simple event is
>   the scope of life:
> let's not make up
> categories to toss ourselves
> around with.

The "forces" to which we are subject, and which we embody, "are / real forces," though differently named in different places, "real forces which we / don't understand":

> I can either believe
> in them or doubt them &
> I believe.
> ....
> thought jails!
> keep us out!

Finally, then, if our vision of nature is sensitive enough to nature's possibilities and we acknowledge mystery, we may come to feel wonder or awe. This feeling, which I take to be the third subject the poem may be said to be "about,"

may even lead to a *credo*, as it does the poet directly after the
final "I believe" above:

> I believe that man is
> small
> & of short duration in the
> great, incomprehensible,
> & eternal: I believe
> it's necessary to do
> good
> as we can best define it:
> I believe we must
> discover & accept the
> > terms
> > that best testify:
> I'm on the side of
> whatever the reasons are
> > we are here:
>
> > we do the best we can
> > & it's not enough.

The religious feeling implied by these lines is sometimes
explicitly argued for as necessary. Even as we treasure the
"real"—not really knowing what it is—we must honor the
"visionary," for

> our existence is
> > evidence
> > of more
> than we can imagine: much
> we can't see
> is working right:
> > let's celebrate
> > that part of our
> > ignorance

> & keep on
> till we learn better how to
> praise:
>
>> will you leave
>> the Lord
>> & sit down
>> in a man-made misery?
>> then
>> you've postulated a lot
>> for yourself
>> & lost:

Despite, then, our inability to know with any certainty "what *is* out there? beyond / the touch of what / we make?" and our suspicion that "reality . . . is indifferent," we may still honestly engage in "praise" and "celebration," which may seem ruled out by the "known" but is permitted by the reality we only half-know:

> if we looked only by
> what we know,
>> we couldn't turn our
>> heads:
>> if we were at the
>> mercy of what
> we understand,
> our eyes couldn't see:
>
>> discovery is
>> praise &
> understanding is
> celebration:

So, while feeling "the bitterness of fate" and recognizing the precariousness of human life, we still know we

> must do what we can,

accept the rest:
God, help us: help us:

we praise Your light:
give us light to do what
we can with darkness:

And so the poet, who has reminded himself and his reader over and over again of the need to face facts squarely and to keep in mind the known mechanisms of living and perceiving, can still, at "the turn of the year," express religious feelings in traditional religious language:

Lord, I'm in your
hands: I surrender:
it's your will
& not mine:
you give me
singing shape
& you turn me to dust:

undefined &
indefinable, you're
beyond reach:

what form should my
praise take?
this long thin
song?

Not surprisingly, later on the same day the poet notes that he feels "a little / shivery" and next day hopes he has not prettified tragedies or "glossed over the / unmistakable evils," wondering,

has panic
tried to make a flower:

then, hope distorts

me:
turns wishes into lies:

With other people and the natural world so conspicuously absent in the poem, except as abstractions, should we
call *Tape for the Turn of the Year* a visionary poem? Not formally, certainly, if our expectations of what a visionary poem
should be like have been formed from the poetic tradition
that began in this country with Whitman. A "meditative
poem" rather, though the varied meditations seem unpre-
meditated ("I wrote about these / days / the way life gave
them: / I didn't know / beforehand what I / wd write"). We
might even be tempted to call it a "philosophic" poem—if
we had not been so often warned of the dangers of traditional
philosophy's way of constructing mental boxes that take us
"out of nature" by relying solely on "mind," defined as pure
reason.

But even as we note the poem's intellectualism, we become aware of a curious sort of parallel with the visionary
poems we have been looking at: the poet in his study is thinking, not perceiving, but the thoughts are typed as they "come
to mind," unprogrammed, prompted by the circumstances
and feelings of the day and by the total context. The specifics
of this poet on this day, feeling this way, reminded of these
particulars of his experience, are, or seem to be, in control,
much as what is seen in the visionary poem gives rise to
vision in a heightened and deepened sense.

Despite the novelty of its form, then, *Tape* has something in common with "A Noiseless Patient Spider." Both
poems offer a way of "coming home,"

a way of
going along with this

world as it is:

nothing ideal: not as
you'd have it

but rich enough with possibility to warrant acceptance and even praise.

★ ★ ★

The relation of *Sphere* to the Whitmanic paradigm of the visionary poem is at once more tenuous and more impressive. In *Tape*, the "unplanned" poem that Ammons would have us believe simply "happened," with the thoughts typed out just as they came to him, the "visionary" impulse finds expression in the traditional religious language of the West and even takes the form of prayers that, out of context, would be orthodox enough but that in the context of all the naturalistic thoughts seem almost to be examples of that "high-falutin language" Ammons would have us avoid. As the lines move back and forth between the quotidian and the transcendent, thought and feeling seem to alternate in control. Still, though the language of the overtly religious passages may be wishful, the feelings expressed by these passages make it clear that *Tape* is in some sense at least related to the visionary tradition, despite almost complete absence in the poem of the world beyond the study walls.

The paradox: though thought seems wholly in control in *Sphere*, the possibility of wonder survives, and in the end there are still "many rafts to ride," despite the fact that the evidence of thought seems to mean that religious vision is not the result of sensitive perception but, rather, is simply "projected." The paradoxes are insisted upon: "To believe what runs against the / evidence," we read, is difficult, requiring "concentration, imagination, stubbornness, / art, and some

magic: the need to disbelieve belief so disbelief can be believed."[3]

Difficult, surely, but apparently not only possible but in
some sense humanly necessary: "here's my credo. . . . when
you come / to know the eternal forces realizing themselves
through form / you will need to lay on no special determination to assent / to what demands none." Only if "truth is
colorless" (as in Stevens' "The Snow Man") do the "fictions /
need [to] be supreme, real supreme with hot-shot convinc-
ingness." There is no need for us to try to imagine a ghost-
haunted world in order to experience religious awe and wonder, or even to nourish religious hope.

After we have read this passage in sections 56 and 57 of
the poem, we are in a position to understand better the implications of what we have already read in the dedicatory
poem "For Harold Bloom," in which the poet says that having found nowhere "the image for *longing*," he "gathered
mud" and with his hands "made an image for *longing*":

> I took the image to the summit: first
> I set it here, on the top rock, but it completed
> nothing: then I set it there among the tiny firs
> but it would not fit:
> so I returned to the city and built a house to set
> the image in
> and men came into my house and said
>   that is an image for *longing*
> and nothing will ever be the same again

His desire to "see straight" and thus achieve a "naked
vision" without any intermixture of fictions, especially su-

---

3 *Sphere: The Form of a Motion* (New York, 1974), 35. All quotations
from *Sphere* are from this edition.

preme fictions, required that he make the image himself rather than accept those that had served in the past; but his need to make it prepares us for the way he later defines his identity not by either his skepticism or his knowledge of scientific facts but by what he can't keep his mind off: "some people when they get up in the morning see / the kitchen sink, but I look out and see the windy rivers / of the Lord in the tree-tops"—a vision for which the only "evidence" required is personal experience. For philosophy, "finely / rational and small," offers no answers to the question that he says keeps returning to him, the question of "how to be saved." The question keeps returning even though he "knows," or thinks he knows, that "redemptions despise reality" and that "to be saved is here, local and mortal."

Sphere is a discussion of what can be believed without illusion when we trust not analytic philosophy but what is implied today by "good science," keep our eyes and minds open to the "radiance" that is available to us when we contemplate the sphere revealed by science equally in the atom and the cosmos, and yet still keep a tight rein on our imaginations. As discussion, *Sphere* is a philosophical poem despite its rejection of contemporary analytic philosophy in favor of the sciences of the microscopic and the macroscopic. For Ammons, it is science, not philosophy or pure thought, that "makes mysticism discussable without a flurry."

Despite occasional images like "the windy rivers / of the Lord in the treetops," the discussion is carried on primarily in the colloquially worded language of propositional statements, with a heavy reliance on a vocabulary drawn from the sciences. But this closeness to prose is balanced by the formal arrangement in 155 sections of four three-line "stanzas," a form at once conspicuously "artificial" (like poetry) and unvarying (like the phenomena described by scientific laws). The form combines the complete predictability of "law" (genetics, for example) with freedom for the discrete units of thought (the "principle of indeterminacy" of quantum physics), that may begin or end anywhere, without regard to line endings or section breaks.

Typically, the lines run on, the "stanzas" run on, and the sections run on, so that both determinacy and indeterminacy are always present. Only the poem as a whole is complete in itself; lines, tercets, and sections run into each other, so that, while the form is fixed, the sense of meaning is free. A typical line like

changed is that in the future we may have the force to keep

forces us to go back to the preceding line (and tercet) to find the subject of "changed" ("what may have") and on to the next line (and tercet) to discover the object of "keep" ("the changes secular"). Depending on how sympathetically we are reading the poem, lines like these will seem to be either arbitrarily chopped-up prose or a poetic form chosen for the way it suggests that "form of a motion" that the poet finds descriptive of the world revealed by science, microscopically and macroscopically.

This tension between the line and its meaning suggests also another theme that runs through the poem, the tension between "facts" and what we make of them, as the way the poem begins and ends on the subject of "love" should make clear. As the opening section moves through opinions, facts, and jokes to the scientific vocabulary that describes love's usefulness as a "drive," it tends to devaluate its subject:

The sexual basis of all things rare is really apparent
and fools crop up where angels are mere disguises:
a penetrating eye (insight), a penetrating tongue (ah),

a penetrating penis and withal a penetrating mind,
integration's consummation: a com- or intermingling of parts,
heterocosm joyous, opposite motions away and toward

along a common line, the in-depth knowledge (a dilly),
the concentration and projection (firmly energized) and
the ecstasy, the pay off, the play out, the expended

nexus nodding, the flurry, cell spray, finish, the
haploid hungering after the diploid condition: the reconciler
of opposites, commencement, proliferation, ontogeny:

In the final section, the unnamed sexual act suggested by
the motions evoked by the images has become a transcendent
experience of being freed, if only briefly, from the limitations
of space, time, and self:

to float the orb or suggest the orb is floating: and, with the
mind thereto attached, to float free: the orb floats, a bluegreen
wonder: so to touch the structures as to free them into rafts

that reveal the tide: many rafts to ride and the tides make a
place to go: let's go and regard the structures, the six-starred
easter lily, the beans feeling up the stakes: we're gliding: we

are gliding: ask the astronomer, if you don't believe it: but
motion as a summary of time and space is gliding us: for a
    while,
we may ride such forces: then, we must get off: but now this

beats any amusement park by the shore: our Ferris wheel,
    what a
wheel: our roller coaster, what mathematics of stoop and
    climb: sew
my name on my cap: we're clear: we're ourselves: we're
    sailing.

The final implication of *Sphere*, then, despite the poet's
repeated and emphatic rejections of any sort of religious

supernaturalism, is that a mechanistic and reductive view of the world cannot appeal to contemporary science for support any more than it can to personal experience, for there's more to the world than meets the scientific eye—and good scientists know it. Although in some moods we can be "glad the emphasis these days / is off dying beautifully and more on light-minded living with / the real things—soap, spray-ons, soda, paper towels, etc.," we are not for long allowed to ignore the secondary meaning of "light" in "light-minded." The light we see by is also, in some visionary sense, "the light of the world," which may be described either as "photons" of radiant energy converted, in a way not understood, to electrical energy in the intelligent eye; or, for other purposes but with equal truth, simply as "radiance."

Whether we talk about photons and electrical impulses or about radiance, we are talking about the same thing, either as it is known to contemporary science or as it may be experienced. Thus the half-joking factual, physiological, and finally generalized and "scientific" description of the sexual act in the first section, presenting sex as it is theoretically and practically "known," leads naturally to the final section's evocation of the same act as "known" in personal experience. Tone, vocabulary, and implications are all altered now. Creatures of earth still, we can regard the "bluegreen / wonder" of the earth as if from space, experience the "structures" becoming "rafts" on which we may ride for a while, and feel, instead of abstractly knowing, the "mathematics of stoop and climb." So the poem that begins with the factual and theoretic ends with a visionary affirmation of transcendence. Love has changed from a biological survival mechanism to something like a gateway to the eternal. The poet's hope to "keep the changes secular" has been fulfilled, and the question he has asked has received an affirmative answer:

. . . can we, accepting
our smallness, bend to cherish the greatness that rolls through
our sharp days, that spends us on its measureless currents: and
so, for a moment, if only for a moment, participate in those
     means

that provide the brief bloom in the eternal presence: is this
our saving: is this our perishable thought that imperishably
bears us through the final loss: then sufficient thanks for that.

★ ★ ★

Tape for the Turn of the Year and *Sphere: The Form of a Motion*
seem to me the long poems by Ammons that bear the clearest
relation to the visionary tradition in American poetry I have
been examining. But there has always been a strong antivisionary current flowing in Ammons' poetry, too, a cautious
skepticism, a fear that the imagination may lead not to a
deeper vision but to the imaginary. In his early work, this
skeptical streak generally seemed only to result in rein-
forcing the poet's conscious determination to keep the changes
secular while still remaining aware of mystery and open to
wonder.

But "Summer Session 1968," first collected in *Uplands*
(1970), seems to me to mark a turning point in Ammons'
career. After this, except for *Sphere* in 1974, the poems will
more often remind us of Harold Bloom, who "discovered"
Ammons, than of Emerson. "Summer Session 1968" equates
the visionary with the imaginary in such a way as to undercut
the visionary poems that preceded it and *Sphere* that would
follow. The mood moves through disillusion to suggest dis-
gust, of which the poet feels the helpless victim: "well I can't
recover the light: / in my head." But if the "light" is in his
head only, then there is no sort of veracity to be found in the
visionary poems I have been discussing. The poet tries to
counter the mood by reminding himself that "scientific ob-

jectivity puts a radiance on duckshit even," but the reminder seems not to help much, for the "scientific" description of lovemaking, with the "mess of bacterial bloomers" present in the vagina, leaves the sexual act seeming unpleasant and perhaps even a little ridiculous. "Knowledge" in this poem is wholly reductive in its effect whenever it "shivers into the bloodstream," internalized and taken seriously. Its ultimate effect is to lead to the thought that "life adds up to exactly nothing."

"Extremes and Moderations" and "Hibernaculum," included in *Collected Poems, 1951–1971*, discuss the poet's craft and his attempts to empty the heart of concern for the world of the senses, without making any concessions to wish. The "lean belief" described in "Hibernaculum" (a protective coating or structure in which to remain dormant for the winter) ought, the poet thinks, to find expression in "the lean word" but issues instead in seemingly endless "considerations":

> to lean belief the lean word comes,
> each scope adjusted to the plausible: to the heart
> emptied of, by elimination, the world, comes the small
>
> cry domesticating the night. . . .
>
> . . . I address the empty place where the god
> that has been deposed lived: it is the godhead: the
> yearnings that have been addressed to it bear antiquity's
>
> sanction: for the god is ever re-created as
> emptiness, till force and ritual fill up and strangle
> his life, and then he must be born empty again:
>
> accost the emptiness saying let all men turn their
> eyes to the emptiness that allows adoration's life:
> that is my whole saying, though I have no intention to
>
> stop talking. . . .

Ammons is still talking in this passage, and explicitly or

implicitly throughout the poem, about what he had said in *Tape* that he couldn't keep his mind off, and also in *Diversifications*, the volume that followed *Sphere* in 1975. But by this time the emptying of the heart of the world is more nearly complete. Between the quince bush and the "illusory" hollyhocks in "Transcendence," which opens the new volume, there is a discernible difference: the quince bush was no illusory product of "Maya," however brief its bloom. But "Transcendence" would have it otherwise. Here is the complete poem:

> Just because the transcendental,
> having digested all change into
> a staying, promises foreverness,
>
> it's still no place to go, nothing
> having survived there into life:
> and here, this lost way, these
>
> illusory hollyhocks and garages,
> this is no place to settle: but
> here is the grief, at least,
>
> constant, that things and loves
> go, and here the love that
> never comes except as permanence.[4]

For Ammons, unlike some of the Zen Buddhist composers of *haiku*, seeing the world of time and space as illusory and conceiving of the eternal as a "permanence" that is Nothingness, the result in the next volume, *The Snow Poems* (1977), is a thick book of verse that I find both trivial and dull. The tension that has lifted so many of the earlier poems is almost wholly relaxed now. There is no more tightrope walking between the subjective and the objective aspects of vision.

4 *Diversifications* (New York, 1975), 1.

Instead, the poet sits, "fifty in the / mid-seventies," contemplating "failing powers" or writes little weather reports verifying the "Forecast for Today," the fact that it "Snowed Last Night a Lot but Warmed Up," and finally, in the last poem in the volume, snow not experienced at all, even through the study window, but merely heard about: "They Say It Snowed."

Now and then the reason for the retreat to the trivial in *The Snow Poems* becomes explicit: "sight / feeds on a / medium / whose / source blinds." But more often it is merely implicit, as it is in those poems that, by including the poet's second thoughts in the margin, at once invite the reader to write his own poem and signal the poet's abandonment of the Ezra role. The poet tells us, marginally, that he'd still "rather be / the flakey / fool of hope / than the / smartass / of the / small and mean," but we find very little now of that "touching, tasting, looking" that once, by seeming to reveal "beauty's unbelievable contrary" of the "trash" we have learned we are, had created the tension that had lifted so many of the earlier poems above the humdrum and made them memorable—a tension that had continued in later poems even when the world of the senses was more thought about than concretely evoked. In a world in which the seen has lost its natural radiance and the unseen has become "unbelievable," poetry comes to seem as empty as hope.

★   ★   ★

Fortunately for those who have cared about his poetry, shortly after I had written the above, *Snow Poems* was followed by a volume that contains several of Ammons' finest poems and, overall, reads both like a return and a fresh start, as though the poet had got his second wind, or, better, like the birds seen on Easter morning, had circled, perhaps looking for an updraft. Confessing himself now a failed visionary whose mood is normally elegiac as he contemplates the wreckage of time and loss, he writes as though he has come through a bad time and learned how to make do with what is left. "I can't regain / the lost idyllic at all, but the woods are here with us." And not only the woods but "the clear particular," which may give "a composure past sight," and neighbors, and "you, lover," can bring the feeling of being "unlost and unbetrayed."

What had betrayed him, "Traveling Shows" seems to me to imply, was his attempt to join company with Ezra in the rebuilding of a temple, new-style, with scientific underpinnings and Eastern religious thought worked into its design:

> I found vision and it
> was terrific, the sight
> enabling and abiding, but
> I couldn't get these
> old bones there and light's
> a byproduct of
> rapid decomposition:
> ....
> . . . I found, I
> found: it was nothing:
> ....
> the real world
> succeeds the made and,
> burnt out, shuts down.[5]

Still, for the time being, before both the "real" and the "made" world shut down, there are "things" that say what cannot be said in words, things that "praise themselves seen

5 *A Coast of Trees* (New York, 1981), 31. All subsequent quotations from Ammons are from this volume.

in / my praising sight," so that a kind of celebration or praise of particular moments or particular things is once again possible even in the absence of the collapsed visionary framework created by reason working with propositions. Now

> I take myself, in
> the goal of my destiny,
> the way the wind takes
> me. . . .
> . . . .
> nothing to nothing:
> but meanwhile my
> body knows the wind and
> calls it out,
> and dust and snow,
> the running brook,
> praise themselves seen in
> my praising sight.

When moments of vision come now, they sometimes come more like "a blade of fire. . . . burning confusion up" than a ray of light. With particulars still holding him and calling for the praise he can no longer articulate, half-ready for the nothing as he is, "ahead the chief / business is tearing the rest / of the way loose." Meanwhile, though too much analysis may make the radiance no longer helpful, there is love, the "greatest of these," as St. Paul said. "Wiring" cannot be excerpted and is short enough to quote entire:

> Radiance comes from
> on high and, staying,
> sends down silk
> lines to the flopping
> marionette, me, but
> love comes from

> under the ruins and
> sends the lumber up
> limber into leaf that
> touches so high it nearly
> puts out the radiance

Although *A Coast of Trees* is made up of short lyrics
(except for "Easter Morning") expressive of varying moods
and discrete insights, with time, "The Fourth Dimension,"
generally dominant, two features of the volume suggest to
me that the failed visionary is not yet through with attempts
at celebration, despite the failure, in his eyes, of his earlier
attempt. First, there is the poem he chose to place last in the
volume, "Persistences." The chief actor in the poem, wind,
has lost any of the suggestion of "spiritus" it had in "Raft"
and now is seen as wearing away the temple in the desert, as
well as wearing away ourselves, but,

> from our own ruins
> we thrash out the
> snakes and mice,
> shoo the lean ass away,
> and plant a row of something:
> ....
> in debris we make a holding as
> insubstantial and permanent as mirage.

"Insubstantial" and "permanent," given equal weight—but
who had supposed that visions were built of weighable, mea-
surable "substance"? "Mirage," at once an optical illusion and
a natural phenomenon—which "truth" we shall emphasize is
up to us.

The other feature of the volume that makes me want to
see it as a volume of recovery is that "Easter Morning," the

longest and greatest poem in the volume, ends on a note of
ambiguous hope, and even of muted "celebration." Before
the two great birds overhead are seen, the tone of the poem
has been one of controlled agony and horror as the poet re-
lives the many deaths of his childhood and anticipates the
deaths to come, as we all "buy the bitter knots of / horror,
silently raving, and go on / crashing into empty ends not /
completions," but the actions of the birds that flew at last out
of sight—something "never seen before"—seems

> a sight of bountiful
> majesty and integrity: the having
> patterns and routes, breaking
> from them to explore other patterns or
> better ways to routes, and then the
> return: a dance sacred as the sap in
> the trees, permanent in its descriptions
> as the ripples round the brook's
> ripplestone: fresh as this particular
> flood of burn breaking across us now
> from the sun.

The sight at least is no "mirage," though the kind of
corroboration it may lend to the "picture-book, letter-
perfect / Easter morning" is left open. The poem says too
perfectly what it "means" for paraphrase to be other than
desecration, but I will risk this comment, not paraphrase
but prompted by it: both death, of all we have loved and still
love, and the onward movement of life till it goes out of sight
are to be taken with equal seriousness.

As I read the poem—perhaps too subjectively—I am reminded not only of the dance of Roethke's "Once More, The
Round" and of the "Desert Music" heard by Williams, but
even of Whitman's pair of late poems, "Grand Is the Seen"

and "Unseen Buds." All these poems imply that the seen and the unseen make a pair, each of which is incomplete without the other.

Ammons has never written so well as he does *A Coast of Trees*. Never before, either, has he shown himself so aware of others—as in "Easter Morning" and in his highly unusual love poem, "Keepsake"—or so aware of the difficulty and cost of vision. It is not only Roethke, Williams, and Whitman who come to mind as I read these poems but even—though the suggestion may seem far-fetched to many and I suspect will not please Ammons himself—the Eliot of *Four Quartets*, especially in the "redemptive suffering" passages and the ending of "The Dry Salvages." Eliot would have understood the implications of Ammons' light that becomes "a blade of fire . . . burning confusion up," his determination to avoid the idyllic, and his concentration on *now*. Ammons is in distinguished company in this volume, which allows us to hope that his visionary quest will continue through many more.

CHAPTER VII

David Wagoner

"Traveling Light"

David Wagoner in his best and most characteristic poems earns the title of "visionary poet," though he would no doubt reject the description, in part for a semantic reason, equating "visionary" with romantic gush, in part because of the honorific associations the word more and more carries in contemporary critical usage. But his most memorable poems—the poems he has gradually learned how to write, nearly all produced in the past decade, the poems that are distinctively his own, demanding to be compared with no other poet's—fit the description of a visionary poem I started out with. So I will call him a visionary poet, whether he likes the description or not.

Visionary, as I have been using the term, has clear religious implications, as it has when applied to Blake, Whitman, Yeats, and other "visionary" poets. (That the word may appropriately be applied to secular thinkers like Marx I take for granted, but that use of the word is not my subject.) And Wagoner, like Whitman and Roethke, and unlike either Eliot or Stevens, is a religious visionary poet in his best work. This despite his frequent repudiations of his religious background, of religious "otherworldliness," and of creeds of all sorts ("Revival," "Trying to Pray," "Boy Jesus," and many others). Despite, too, his consistently empirical and skeptical stance: living in the ruins, making our way with difficulty in broken country, misled by reflections and optical illusions, unable to reach any certainty not only about any "absolutes" but even about "matter of fact." If the "real" world lies beyond or behind our world, the world of our experience, we cannot in any strict sense of the word really *know* it. Yet Wagoner is still a religious visionary poet in the same sense that, for those who have had the patience and the stamina to read through to the end of *Process and Reality*, with its final chapter on "God and the World," Whitehead may be called a religious philosopher.

Wagoner is a visionary poet whose work invites the description "naturalist"—in two of that much-abused word's quite different senses, that which would apply to Whitehead and that which would fit John Muir or John Burroughs. We are a part of nature, and nature is in us as well as around us. Nature—the natural world, the nonmanmade—is our proper study. But Wagoner's "naturalism" has very little in common with the naturalism of the late nineteenth and early twentieth centuries—one thing only, really, and that is the denial that we are separate from nature, "specially created," differently made. The "naturalist" perspective in his work carries no traces of the mechanism that worried Robinson, the materialism that Jeffers at first accepted and later tried to escape, or the positivism that Williams seems at times to have thought he believed in and that Eliot repudiated so radically.

But of course Whitman and Roethke were "naturalists" also in the sense that applies to Wagoner, so that there is nothing wholly new about his kind of naturalism. Rather, he seems their truest heir, closer to Whitman than Ammons is, closer than any other poet I know of writing today to Roethke. Heir perhaps, but not follower or disciple. Having found his own voice, his own point of view, and his own best subjects, he is necessarily *unlike* Whitman, Roethke, and the others in all sorts of ways. Probably he learned the most from Roethke, whose student he once was and whose notebooks he has edited but no one would be likely to mistake one of his major poems for a poem by Roethke, even when the two treat similar subjects. He simply carries on from Whitman and Roethke as a different person, and so as a different poet, in a different age.

Wagoner is unlike Whitman, for example, not only because of the gap that separates the language, sensibility, and intellectual climate of Whitman's time from ours but also because Wagoner's response to urban life and technological culture is mostly negative and his response to the natural world more detailed and seemingly objective than Whitman's, even while remaining equally positive. "The rolling earth" seems an imaginatively prophetic idea in Whitman's poems, a seen, felt, known, sometimes frightening fact in Wagoner's. The ecological health of the planet seems secure in Whitman's poems, threatened by "progress" and profit in Wagoner's. Again, human danger, privation, suffering are nearer the surface in Wagoner's poems. There is no need to go on: there is not much point in comparing, on so abstract a level, two poets so far separated in time, temper, and outlook. Their differences are obvious at a glance, their similarities apparent only on a very high level of abstraction. A century of war and suffering, loss of hope and loss of belief, the holocaust and the atomic revolution have intervened.

But Wagoner is also unlike the other poets I have treated who are closer to him in time. He seems not to suffer from Crane's psychic torments or the painful bifurcation of the world into subway and bridge that Crane tried to overcome but could not. He does not appear to believe, as Crane apparently did, that reality can be apprehended only in mystic (poetic?) vision or in transport or myth. Unlike Williams, for most of his life, he does not suppose that the world of fact presents itself to us unambiguously, so that one need be only a "realist" to see that there are "no ideas but in things": he knows, as many do now, that "seeing," in the sense of recognizing and relating, necessarily involves interpreting and even what might be called a degree of "projecting"—that the experimenter, in short, cannot be left out of the experiment. (But in more confident moods he can still write, "I see what to say.") Unlike Ammons, he is not hung up on the insoluble philosophic problem of the relation of the One and the many. Nor is he, like Williams as well as Ammons, involved in the effort to avoid the "poetic": his poetry makes no pretence of just "happening."

In short, he seems to me the first poet I have treated who is truly a poet of our time yet still has not, like the Ammons of *Snow Poems*, given up the visionary hope, or reduced it to a mere nostalgia or solipsism, as so many of our contemporary poets have done. Writing after Whitehead and the Existentialists, in a post-Existential time that calls for waiting to see, he can find nourishment for the visionary in the visual, even in this time of threat to all life on this planet. His visionary poems revise but do not betray Whitman's "Song of the Rolling Earth."

★ ★ ★

Wagoner's first several volumes give the impression of being the work of a "traditional," highly competent, but not strikingly original poet who is not, like Williams, and even Ammons in his vertical verse, "antimodernist" but postmodernist, well beyond the modernist rejection of the nineteenth century. We might suppose, reading most of the poems in these early volumes, that Rimbaud and Eliot, Symbolism, "free verse," and Williams' rejection of the "poetic" had never occurred. Traditional subjects in traditional forms hold our attention not by any radical experimentation but by the skill with which common words are used in uncommon ways to express time-honored feelings and impressions. This poet, we may feel, has unusual sensitivity to words and knows that they are what the poet works with, but he has not yet put his

personal stamp on them: the poems seem the work of a skill-
ful craftsman whose thoughts and experiences are so like our
own that any one of a number of poets might have written
them—or even we ourselves if we had sufficient skill with
words.

But rather quickly, reading on, we discover several qualities in the work that set it apart from the bulk of highly
competent verse treating themes that are commonplace in
modern literature. In place of either formal experimentation
or novelty of outlook we are aware of tone in the poems,
aware that when they impress us most, the tone is what distinguishes them. Then we begin to see also that this poet of
the tried-and-true not only dares to treat common subjects in
common language arranged in pre-Modernist forms, even to
using occasional rhyme, but actively seeks out worn everyday expressions to make us hear them for the first time, re-
freshed and renewed in a context that prompts us to take
them as seriously as we take statements of fact.

This poet has decided, he says, to use "the old words" in
ways that will make us look again at the experiences they
must have called up before they became dead metaphors. So
we read "stood its ground," "in the bag," "key men," "on the
table," "head over heels," "to fatten them up for the kill,"
"sunnyside up," "forgive my trespasses," "under their own
steam," "humdrum lives," "being taken in," "biting the
dust," "its level best," "won't hold water," "closing time,"
"knocking on wood"—worn phrases out of everyday talk,
given fresh meaning by a recollection of the literal, or else
literalisms that conceal forgotten deeper meanings. Some of
the poems in Wagoner's first several volumes seem to exist
only for and by virtue of this verbal play related to punning.
Reading them and remembering only the word-plays, I re-

mind myself that art is, among other things, a form of play, that, despite Emerson's advice and Whitman's practice, the poet need not be a seer or prophet, and that wit is not to be despised.

But when we come to "A Guide to Dungeness Spit" in Wagoner's second volume, *Nesting Ground,* all such reminders not to expect too much come to seem unnecessary and irrelevant. This is a major poem by any standard and the first that we can imagine no other poet of our time having written. In it, the voice we hear not only is content with "the old words" but demands to be taken as literally as we would take the directions in a guidebook, or the words of a professional guide leading a guided tour. "Those . . . are Canada geese; / Some on the waves are loons, / And more on the sand are pipers."[1] We follow and are told what it is we are seeing, needing to be told because we are city-born and unfamiliar with the earth. "Let us step this way. Follow me closely / Past snowy plovers bustling among sand-fleas." As we approach the end of the spit and look back at the land behind us, we find that the once-taken-for-granted has become strange, needing to be identified by our guide as the birds and the shells on the sand have been: "Those are called houses, and those are people." These objects too are a part of the nature we have been exploring, and as such need to be identified when seen from this distance, from the far end of the spit, where we are close to the sea.

"A Guide to Dungeness Spit" is Wagoner's first "visionary poem," and a very distinguished one. It would be followed in later volumes by many others like it, to become the

1 *Collected Poems, 1956–1976* (Bloomington, Ind., 1978), 20. Unless otherwise indicated, all subsequent quotations from Wagoner's verse are from this volume.

poet's most important contribution to our poetry. The movement in it is ultimately from sight to insight, from the outward to the inward, from nature to man and then to man-in-nature, fusing the inward and outward, subjective and objective.

The refreshment of vision the poem affords is related to, but beyond, the verbal play we have noted as a Wagoner characteristic. There is only one example of what could be called, pejoratively, "clever word-play" in the poem: "spit and image" near the end, which I find a flaw that ought to have been avoided. But it is the only reminder that this is an early poem—a pun we could do without, for its point has already been made. But even this didactic witticism cannot spoil so fresh and memorable a poem. The voice we hear in "A Guide to Dungeness Spit," speaking knowledgeably of matters of fact, yet opening up vistas that reveal unsuspected possibilities as we "climb to the light in spirals, / And look" from the lighthouse at the end of the spit, at what we have seen without taking in all our lives, seen as too familiar to prompt wonder, seen without seeing from this perspective—this voice will be heard often again in the poet's finest and most original poems. The most distinctive quality of the voice is suggested by the fact that it could with equal justice be described as "neonaturalistic" and "neo-Transcendental."

★ ★ ★

In our time, a poet who would guide us to a rediscovery of our source and a fresh recognition of how similar our condition is to that of our remote ancestors, human and prehuman, and do so primarily in poems devoted to experience in nature, cannot easily avoid being dismissed by urban or exurbanite readers as a neoromantic "nature poet" whose vision is shaped more by nostalgia for what is disappearing and threatened than by a realistic assessment of present-day experience and possibilities. How can he be taken seriously by readers who have never been lost in the wilderness or faced a bear? Wagoner is, I would guess, acutely aware of this problem and deals with it in two ways: first, by writing a good deal of verse, often "light verse," about subjects that have nothing to do with nature and do not suggest the "visionary," either formally or thematically; second, by keeping his defenses up, like the early Ammons, as he writes of how to discover what and where we are in the universe—that is, in "nature," the cosmos, that uncontrolled, illimitable, and ultimately uncontrollable reality we briefly inhabit.

In his visionary nature poems, Wagoner guards himself—whether consciously or unconsciously, I do not know—in three ways, as I see it. First, he shows himself aware of the "mechanics" of literal vision and so of the biologically built-in ambiguities of visual perception. Without ever appearing to be reflecting, Ammons-fashion, on the implications of scientific theory, he frequently makes it clear that common experiences reveal the limitations and subjectivity of vision. Let us look at just two quite different examples of this. In the early poem "On seeing an X-Ray of My Head," he writes,

> Accept at your ease
> Directly what was yours at one remove:
> Light through your eyes,
> Air, dust, and water as themselves at last. Keep smiling.
> Consider the source.

Again, in a very different vein, he writes in a way that makes it clear that what is seen is *being seen* by someone, even in the poems that could be described as simply descriptive. In his most recent volume, *Landfall*, "Nuthatch" describes a common bird often seen at feeders, but not the *Ding-an-sich* of the bird, rather, the "bird as seen," not the bird known, or known about, classified, dissected. The result is a description that seems at once accurate and empathic, "realistic" without any pretense of neutral "objectivity." Observer and bird are both present in the poem:

> Quick, at the feeder, pausing
> Upside down, in its beak
> A sunflower seed held tight
> To glance by chestnut, dust-blue,
> White, an eye-streak
> Gone in a blurred ripple
> Straight to the cedar branch
> To the trunk to a crevice
> In bark and putting it
> In there, quick, with the others,
> Then arrowing straight back
> For just one more all morning.[2]

A second line of defense (almost certainly not so conceived by the poet) is Wagoner's habit of looking down before he looks up, of paying meticulous attention to the "facts" before trying to see what meanings they imply, especially if there is any possible suggestion of transcendence involved in them. Emerson in "Two Rivers" had glanced quickly at the actual river in his first two lines, then gone on about the transcendent river for eighteen more. Wagoner's "neo-Transcendental" practice very nearly reverses Emerson's emphasis. "An Offering for Dungeness Bay" seems so like a paradigm of Wagoner's visionary nature poems, and would suffer so much from paraphrase, that I shall quote it

2   *Landfall* (Boston, 1981), 24.

entire despite its length, saying about it only this: note that
the movement is down before it is up.

1

The tern, his lean, slant wings
Swiveling, lifts and hovers
Over the glassy bay,
Then plunges suddenly into that breaking mirror,
Into himself, and rises, bearing silver
In his beak and trailing silver
Falling to meet itself over and over.

2

Over the slow surf
Where the moon is opening,
Begin, the plover cries,
And beyond the shallows
The far-off answer,
Again, again, again,
Under the white wind
And the long boom of the breakers
Where the still whiter branches
Lie pitched and planted deep,
Only begin, the water says,
And the rest will follow.

3

Dusk and low tide and the sanderlings
Alighting in their hundreds by the last of the light
On seawrack floating in the final ripples
Lightly, scarcely touching, and now telling
This night, *Here*, and this night coming,
Here, where we are, as their beaks turn down and thin,
As fine as sandgrains, *Here is the place.*

4

The geese at the brim of darkness are beginning

To rise from the bay, a few at first in formless
Clusters low to the water, their black wings beating
And whistling like shorebirds to bear them up, and
     calling
To others, to others as they circle wider
Over the shelving cove, and now they gather
High toward the marsh in chevrons and echelons,
Merging and interweaving, their long necks turning
Seaward and upward, catching a wash of moonlight
And rising further and further, stretching away,
Lifting, beginning again, going on and on.

Finally, under the heading of what I have called Wagoner's "lines of defense," there are the many poems explicitly
disclaiming any "visionary" intent, or even interest. Over
and over the poet insists that he is a hard-headed, down-to-
earth realist with his feet on the ground, no idle dreamer or
victim of illusions. He announced in his first volume, in
"Spring Song," his awareness of living in the fragmented
world described by Henry Adams, in which invoking the
myths—using God-language as Roethke had late in his career—had come to seem impossible and in which the only
"spring song" would have to take the form of nonsense
verse.

Twenty years later, in "Ode to the Muse on Behalf of a
Young Poet" (*In Broken Country*), Wagoner mocks the young
poet's reliance on poetic inspiration, his delusion that the
"Sparks, Flashes, and Sudden Leaps / From the Visionary
Aether" have some sort of noetic value as examples of what
Hart Crane had called "the logic of metaphor." The poem is
a good example of Wagoner's light verse, witty, unpreten-
tious, wryly funny in its verbal play—but self-protective,
too, since dependence on the Muse of poetic inspiration is

conspicuous by its absence among the "young poets" who are fashionable today and taken seriously by the reviewers and critics. The description might possibly be altered to fit the Jungians, but there is no indication in the poem that *they* are the ones the speaker has in mind. The poem seems to have more point if the thrust of it is seen as directed against romantic gush in itself rather than against any young poet whose name is likely to come to mind. In any case, whoever the deluded young poet may be thought to be, the meaning Wagoner attributes to "visionary" is clear: "having the nature of fantasies or dreams . . . not practicable at present; idealistic; utopian," as one dictionary puts it. When the young poet grows to maturity, he will come to realize that a poet is a craftsman whose products are fashioned from words.

But would a poet whose deepest concern was only with facticity and craft be moved so often to insist on his "realism"? What I suspect encourages this aspect of the poet's public persona is anxiety lest the "new light" in which the poems let us see things may be judged romantic or wishful because it is found chiefly in poems dealing with nature, not with urban life or technological culture. Have not Modernist art and much recent philosophy made it clear that any patterns of meaning and value we think we find in nature we have really constructed ourselves? Can a poet who finds the wilderness surrounding Stevens' jar in Tennessee not "slovenly" but meaningful and satisfying be taken seriously?

★   ★   ★

The kinds of meanings Wagoner finds in his wilderness experiences quickly become apparent when we start reading his nature poems, beginning with "A Guide to Dungeness Spit," in which we are invited to take a closer, more attentive look at what we find on our walk to the land's end. With the ocean at our backs, we can see that our problem today is what it has always been, "Staying Alive": ("It's temporary. / What occurs after / Is doubtful"). Thinking of ourselves "by time and not by distance" is likely to help us toward "calming down" when we feel we are lost. Even in our "Night Passage" we may see lights "over the water" and "coming on in the dark," if only in the eyes of animals reflecting light from somewhere outside. While we live, we find ourselves engaged in "Crossing Half a River," "living and dying" at once, now and then dreaming ourselves across. Like spawning salmon, we come back to our starting-point in "Riverbed" "with the same unreasoning hope" and "lie down all day beside them"—the fish that have spawned and died.

Post-Modernist though his poetry must be judged to be, Wagoner's nature poems often imply judgments of our culture that align him with the Eliot of *The Waste Land* more than with Williams. Without suggesting that we are in a cultural wasteland, he writes often of the fear of being "Lost," "In the Middle of Nowhere" as it seems, so that we need the tacked-up sign cautioning us, "Do Not Proceed Beyond This Point Without a Guide." (A sufficient "guide" is close at hand, if we will notice it: the hemlock that, without changing locations, "grew up and down at the same time, branch and root.") Our greatest danger may be our preoccupation with our own anxiety.

"The Bad Fisherman" and "Talking to Barr Creek," placed together in *Collected Poems*, offer both caution and the possibility of hope. The fisherman who caught nothing had let his shadow fall on the water, but the speaker who, "like a fool," sits talking to Barr Creek as though it were a "you," "begging a favor, / A lesson," learns something about "going yet staying, being / Born, vanishing, enduring," so that though the anxiety will remain, the hope of not falling apart as we confront both "sweet-afterdeath" and "bittersweet nightshade" can remain alive. However foolish it may be to sit "talking" to Barr Creek, the act seems to be satisfying, whereas in "Trying to Pray" the speaker, unable to see in "the votive darkness," can only reach out hands that "touch what will not answer."

The religious implications of these poems and many others like them should make it clear enough that this poet is *not* concerned only with facts and word-craft but with finding the limits of what can be said meaningfully about our ultimate concerns. Clearly, he is at pains to avoid seeming to be one of the poets characterized in "A Room with a View" as "straining for height," poets who "mistake the roaring in their ears for the ocean."

★ ★ ★

The meaning of the hope suggested by "born, vanishing, enduring" becomes clearer in "Tracking" and "From Here to There," two of the nine impressive poems treating experience in the wild that open *New Poems* (1976). The fact that for most of us today literal tracking is a lost art in no way makes these poems seem exotic: all aware and thoughtful people are engaged in their own kind of "tracking," just as none of us can wholly avoid wondering at times how we can get from here to there. What gives all the poems in the group their distinctiveness is their faithfulness to the literal while raising the largest questions we can ask.

In "Tracking," the "other" whose trail we are trying to follow has left a number of small clues to the direction he has taken, clues discoverable if we are attentive and perceptive enough. If he wanted not to be followed, he has been "careless," for his "heelmarks" may be seen and he has broken the otherwise "dead silence" in which we would find ourselves and disturbed "the natural disorder." At first (in biblical times?) he did not hide his tracks as he might have, so that, using guesswork as well as our eyes, we may still discern his traces. But then his traces become harder to follow and it seems as though he were deliberately trying to elude his tracker by walking on bare rock and in streams. Going upstream when we find that the track has completely vanished, we remember that "everything human / Climbs as it runs away and goes to ground later." We should be prepared to come upon him unexpectedly in an "unwelcome meeting" with

> The other, staring
> Back to see who's made this much of his footprints,
> To study your dead-set face
> And find out whether you mean to kill him, join him,
> Or simply to blunder past.

The solitary hiker we listen to in "From Here to There" is in the mountains of the West where, in the clear air, "distant objects often seem close at hand / When looked at grimly." Making due allowance for the ever-present possibility of visual illusion, he knows that

> Though you can see in the distance, outlined precisely
> With speechless clarity, the place you must go,
> The problem remains
> Judging how far away you are and getting there safely.

Between the speaker and his objective, "(so sharply in focus / You have to believe in them with all your senses) / Lies a host of mirages" that must be understood for what they are, though "light shifts, fidgets, and veers in ways clearly beyond you," making it almost impossible to distinguish the subjective and the objective, desire and fact. Still, speaking from his own experience, the hiker encourages us to believe that

At last, watching your step, having shrugged off most illusions,
And stumbling close enough to rap your knuckles
Against the reality
Of those unlikely rocks you've stared at through thick and thin
Air and the dumb-shows of light, your hope should be,
As a hardened traveller,
Not to see your trembling hands passing through cloud-stuff,
Some flimsy mock-up of a world spun out of vapor,
But to find yourself
In the Land behind the Wind where nothing is the matter
But you, brought to your knees, an infirm believer
Asking one more lesson.

The patience, endurance, and attentiveness required of the hiking "infirm believer" if he is to make it "From Here to There" after he has "shrugged off most illusions" seem demanded by two conflicting emotions and states of mind that are explicit in "Tracking" and "Being Shot" and implicit in this poem: the anxiety produced by imagining your death alone in the woods, and the hope that doing so may allow you to start "seeing things / In a new light" when the "stranger" who may or may not "grant mercy" makes his appearance and you find, unlike Job, that you have nothing to offer him but "your empty hands, now red as his hat." Clearly, for this specimen of *homo viator*, traveling light does not require a total writing-off of all aspects of his religious heritage. What may be necessary instead is suggested in a poem in his latest volume, "Turning Back and Starting Over":

Though we gave ourselves a name when we began—Explorers—

Now, starting over, we have two more to carry:
Backtrackers, Beginners.[3]

★   ★   ★

Wagoner's contribution to the tradition of the visionary poem
in America has been made in his many poems treating experience in nature more concretely and more realistically than
Whitman, less subjectively than Roethke, poems that explore
the natural world and our relation to it without apparent
preconceptions or psychic idiosyncracies. Whitman's vision
of nature is shaped in part by his inheritance of Emerson's
Transcendental ideas, and Roethke's preoccupation with the
greenhouse world of youth and his identification with "the
small" leads us back into biography—though of course without ceasing to be generally meaningful. Crane's use of nature
turns it into a symbol that often works better if not looked at
carefully, whereas most of Williams' excursions beyond the
human and the urban tend to be either Imagistic or abstract.
Ammons in midcareer seemed to be turning away from concrete nature as it could be observed and experienced in a walk
to reflect on the relation of the finite many to the infinite One
as conceived in scientific and philosophic theory and intuited
in Eastern thought: perceivable nature in *The Snow Poems*
takes the form chiefly of weather bulletins and notes on what
can be seen from his study window.

   In Wagoner's visionary nature poems, literal nature is
both the starting point of the poem and the immediate source
of the reflections toward which the poem normally moves.
In his best poems, Wagoner seems Crane's opposite number:
nature is recognized as hard, irreducible, unyielding "fact"
before its metaphoric possibilities "dawn on" the poet and

3   *Ibid.*, 92.

reader. Nature is first of all the "real," the "objective" world "out there," neither created by our technology nor produced by our wishes. Neither plastic nor iron, it is experienced as both limitation and possibility. Although it often leaves us doubtful of where we are, what we should do, and what we can believe, yet it provides sufficient grounds for hope that, if we make a fresh start, try again, we may find ourselves further along toward where we wanted to be, at home in a world that has room for us to move about in, a world of facts that do not exclude transcendence.

The last long poem in Wagoner's most recent volume, "A Sea Change"—one of his most ambitious, with its six-part meditative form—suggests that this hope not only persists but grows even stronger after the exposure to the unknown and the illimitable that has been provided by a sea voyage beyond all familiar landmarks. But keeping the hope alive will require continuous effort

> to learn
> Once more how to point at the trees and birds and animals
> We see around us, even our own hearts,
> Naming, renaming them.[4]

---

4   *Ibid.*, 112.

CHAPTER VIII

Prospects

Apart from the poems still to come from Ammons and Wagoner, what sort of future may we expect for visionary poems of the type I have been tracing from Whitman on? Poetry, like the other arts, is subject to fashions that come and go. With "Modernism" in poetry now a part of recent history, should we expect the same fate for visionary poetry? What would a look at the poetry of the recent past and the present, apart from the work of Ammons and Wagoner, suggest, in this time of ever-more-rapid social and cultural change?

As I look back over the poetry of the past thirty years or so, three poetic movements seem to demand attention. The thoroughgoing rejection of contemporary culture and its philosophic assumptions, already foreshadowed by Pound, Eliot, and Frost, each in his own way, became the task of three "schools" of poets young enough never to have been "Modernists": the "Beats," the "Black Mountain" school, and the "Deep Image" poets, in succession. Each group has seemed to bear some relation to Whitman, to Whitman through Williams, or to the search for a new, nonculturally dominated vision that would allow the rediscovery of personal meaning. None of these movements seems to me to have been lastingly successful in its attempt.

Of the "Beats" welcomed and sponsored by Williams as they turned away from Eliotic "High Culture" and tradition to seek fresh values "on the road," only the verse of Allen Ginsberg, long since driven beyond poetry to drugs and meditation, retains any interest, and that chiefly as an updated expression of some of Whitman's opinions:

> Holy! Holy! Holy! Holy! Holy! Holy! Holy! Holy! Holy!
>   Holy! Holy! Holy! Holy! Holy! Holy!
> The world is holy! The soul is holy! This skin is holy! the nose
>   is holy! the tongue and cock and hand and asshole holy!

Everything is holy! everybody's holy! everywhere is holy!
  everyday is in eternity! Everyman's an angel!
The bum's as holy as the seraphim! the madman is holy as you
  my soul are holy!
The typewriter is holy the poem is holy the voice is holy the
  hearers are holy the ecstasy is holy![1]

Since Ginsberg chose to write as a prophet, presumably he must be thought of as at least a first cousin of Emerson's and Whitman's Seer, but his poems rarely help us to "see" better, allow what has not been seen to dawn on us, too, so that we can see what we had not before noticed. Rather, when they still seem rewarding, it is moral fervor that strikes us: the society emerging in the fifties, after the Second World War, really did bring many of the sensitive to despair or suicide, in either case beyond poetry.

The influence of Williams and Whitman is even more apparent and, if anything, even more unfortunate, in the "projective verse" of Charles Olson and his Black Mountain school. Olson's theory contains nothing new for those who have read their Emerson and Whitman, and his "Maximus" poems seem directly inspired by *Paterson* and *The Cantos*, but though "Olson's push" was meant to reinstate the poet as Seer, his verse seems controlled by abstractions and once read is easily forgotten. Taking his cue from Whitehead's *Process and Reality*, which he seems to have read very selectively, and, like Ammons, from post-Einsteinian science, he often *talked* like a visionary poet, as I have been using the term. He says, for instance, that he is interested in "direct perception," which is "post-logical," so that it can take us out of the box that

1   Allen Ginsberg, *Howl and Other Poems* (San Francisco, 1956), 21 ("Footnote to Howl").

Newtonian science and traditional dualistic language have put us in and restore us to the mythic consciousness and wholeness that primitive people enjoyed before Jewish religion and Greek philosophy merged to produce the culture we must escape from. "I'm bugged mostly by the past. Christ. To get rid of it. To get on."

But where it is we are to get on to does not become clear when we read the "Maximus" poems. Not to present-day Gloucester, certainly. Perhaps to Gloucester as it might have been, but that too remains impossible to envision, though as we read through the *Selected Writings* we hear much about "organism" and "environment" and the mutual interdependence of the two. "Process" *is* "reality" and reality process, we seem to be meant to infer, as though in drawing on Whitehead's book Olson had failed to get as far as Whitehead's final section, in which "flux" is discovered to be only half the picture. At any rate, for this or some other reason, neither persons nor places can be seen in the poems—at any rate as I read them. Both of Olson's poetic heroes, Pound and Williams, wrote better.

After the Beats and the Black Mountain poets, we have had, and still have, the new "Surrealists" or "Deep Image" poets, with Robert Bly leading the way. They seem, at first glance, closer to the visionary tradition I have been tracing than their predecessors are. Bly, for instance, opens one of his collections with an epigraph that begins, "There is an old occult saying: whoever wants to see the invisible has to penetrate more deeply into the visible," and another with a quotation from the mystic Jakob Boehme calling for the two languages needed for dealing with the outward world and the inward world in which we all live. Images drawn from the visible or "outward" world abound in Bly's poetry and that of the others, and instead of Olson's preoccupation with getting rid of the past we encounter nostalgia for it. But the deeper penetration into the visible turns out to be a turning away from it, away from the waking shared world to the world of dream. The world that can be seen is important only as the starting point of a journey into the depths of the psyche, the unconscious, where, as Jung taught, religion and magic still seem real and myth still has meaning. That "Christ will return," can apparently still be dreamed, if not believed.

But when occult revelations granted only in dreams are the subject of poetry, the poems that result can hardly be other than very subjective and are likely to be private. When the images from the outward world must not be visualized but read as hieroglyphs that have meaning only in dream, the world outside the mind is not being transcended but rejected, not penetrated but translated. (Jung tried to warn us against such subjectivism by calling for "individuation," but the surrealist poets seem to ignore the warning.) The free-floating "transcendence" of the actual found so often in much contemporary poetry can as legitimately lead us into the world of nightmare as into a dream of a more meaningful life.

The mood of the poet seems the only determining factor when, as Robert Bly writes, "dreams press us on all sides" and we can choose whether to contemplate "the dying bull . . . bleeding on the mountain" or, "moving inward," the objects that lie "untouched / By the blood. . . . inside the mountain." If the two worlds remain so separate, it is difficult to see how the inward can transform the outward. If we choose to call the poetry of the deep image "visionary," we are using that word in a sense that applies better to Poe than to Whitman. Such poetry seems to me to widen the gap between "to see" and "to envision," not to narrow it, with the result that perception becomes not a mode of discovery but in effect a mode of escape.

★   ★   ★

A great deal of the verse we can read today in the little mag-
azines and the slim paperback volumes seems to have given
up on the world around us and retreated to a concern only
with the dying self and its inner sensations and fears, so that
it is at least conceivable that "expiration," not "inspiration,"
may come to seem the only honest metaphor for life to future
poets. But a line of Roethke's comes to mind and seems to
me perhaps a better indicator of what we may expect: "In a
dark time, the eye begins to see." It is not only Ammons and
Wagoner who have recently written and are writing visionary
poems but many others. Denise Levertov learning to taste
and see, Gary Snyder pondering the ways of life and death in
Turtle Island's wild places, John Haines on his Alaska home-
stead, and, more recently, William Everson trying to penetrate "the masks of drought," Lawrence Lieberman taking
the measurements of the god's image, Robert Pack watching
his daughter in the light, Mary Oliver responding to nature,
and Peter Balakian relishing sense experience and rediscov-
ering the meaning of family history—all these and other
poets have written and are writing poems that have formal
visionary qualities and express visionary attitudes, poems
that find meaning and value in concrete personal experience
of the way things are, or what they are, or may be seen to be.

That it should be, for these and many other poets, not
present society or either high or popular culture but chiefly
Eastern religion or Amerind myth, or else private, wilderness, or family experience that finds expression in poems we
may call visionary is not really surprising when we consider
the nature of our times. With life as we have known it on this
planet threatened by technology—nuclear fission and the
Bomb—and by the population explosion, with our older cities dying and the popular culture purveyed by the media

increasingly dehumanizing, visionary experience of the sort that finds expression in visionary poems seems inauthentic or merely contrived except outside the circles of the quotidian. Values to live by today must be discovered in the most uncrowded places, in nature, space, the new physics, the old faith—almost anywhere but in the marketplace.

But we are not the first to experience dearth and to feel we have to search out new values outside our culture. The English Romantic poets anticipated much of what seems to be going on in our best poetry today, as Thoreau, when he was neither Transcendentalizing to shock his neighbors nor counting the rings on tree stumps, often seems to be foreshadowing the conclusions of contemporary vision researchers about how we must learn to see. Emerson and Whitman looked eastward for religious nourishment before Thomas Merton and Gary Snyder did. The threats we face and the fears we have to live with seem to us to be new in degree, but they are not in kind. As Robert Frost once wrote, "One age is like another for the soul."

★　★　★

A poet's metaphors, which give us what he sees as he sees it and are central to poetry, can retain meaning for us and convey truth even when we find ourselves unable to share the conclusions the poet may draw from them. As Weizsäcker has put it in *The Unity of Nature*, commenting on the distinction between "information" and "truth,"

> Not every linguistic form is information. Information presupposes unambiguousness. Heraclitus' saying that war is the father of all things can be a deep truth for the very reason that it is not information, and it cannot be information because the terms "father" and "war" are not unambiguous. In fact, if they meant what they normally mean, the saying would be nonsensical. But

these terms are also not simply redefined so as to be valid speculative concepts in the philosophy of Heraclitus. A better explanation is that ambiguity is an essential ingredient in any speculative concept used correctly. Surely the meaning of the saying in our example, as it slowly dawns on us, forces the terms into their multiple meanings, thereby hinting at that real relation among the different meanings of a single term which we must perceive in order to understand the whole saying.[2]

Thus, for instance, we need not share the specifics of Whitman's belief in personal immortality to find his best visionary poems still speaking to us powerfully and meaningfully as they affirm life, or subscribe to Zen Buddhist beliefs to find Gary Snyder's best poems helping us to learn to see what we have not seen before. Visionary poems assume the possibility of the transcendence of the quotidian, but such an assumption seems more like an experience—often rare, to be sure—than like a propositional statement of belief, to be affirmed or denied. Crane's "logic of metaphor" retains a kind of validity, though changing "logic" to "felt truth" or "intuition" would help to avoid confusing different kinds of knowledge. The fact that visionary poems "prove" nothing and convey no unambiguous "information," while it may remind us that mystery remains regarding all that is most important to us in life, should not be taken to mean that they offer us no knowledge at all. They offer us the kind of knowledge that comes from seeing and seeing as, and so can enrich our lives, making them seem more meaningful.

In the years that have passed between Whitman's seeing leaves of grass as perhaps "the handkerchief of the Lord," perhaps "the beautiful uncut hair of graves," enough poems of the sort that discover such metaphoric meanings in the

2 C. F. von Weizsäcker, *The Unity of Nature*, trans. Francis J. Zucker (New York, 1980), 41.

perceptible world have been written to justify our thinking of them as a special poetic genre. And if, as I began by suggesting, such thinkers as Barrett and Bateson offer clues to the direction that philosophic thought is taking as we leave naïve positivism behind, then the genre is not likely soon to seem an outdated form. Although the times seem as unpropitious for the poetic rediscovery of many aspects of Whitman's vision today as they proved to be for Crane, poets have lived through bad times before without losing the ability to discover in experience sufficient reasons to keep hope alive. No doubt future readers will continue to prefer "poets of reality," but poets are among those who help us to recognize those features of reality that tend to elude ordinary logic and ordinary language. To rephrase Blake, we see both with and through the eye. Old visions dissolve and are reborn with new features, but it remains true that "where there is no vision, the people perish."

Whatever our religious commitment or lack of it may be, the words of an old children's hymn seem to me pertinent at this point, if we are to avoid solipsism, nihilism, or despair:

O Master, lend us sight
To see the towers gleaming in the light.

APPENDIX

Seeing and Believing

Dickinson, Frost, Eliot, Stevens

At issue throughout this discussion of visionary poetry are two questions: whether the perceived world outside the mind is knowable or unknowable, and whether, if knowable, it is meaningful or meaningless. If it is either unknowable or meaningless, then *visionary* and *illusory* are close synonyms and Wallace Stevens' "Sea Surface Full of Clouds" may properly be called a visionary poem dramatizing the discovery that the values apparently perceived by the innocent eye looking at the sea are really imposed on it, just imagined, not discovered in it. In each of the poem's five sections, the ocean—a sample of "nature," the world—is characterized as a "machine of ocean." The blue we think we see in the ocean is in the eye of the beholder, the result of a transfiguration of a neutral, colorless, or at least unknowable, reality. To perceive is not to discover but either to transform or to impose. The "poem of pure reality," content to "seek nothing beyond reality," will recognize this fact and be content with it, Stevens would write later in "An Ordinary Evening in New Haven." Early and late, Stevens seems to me too much the victim of the scientific world-view that Whitehead described and demolished to be included in the visionary tradition I have been tracing.

If the world outside the mind is essentially knowable and meaningful, then Whitman's "Crossing Brooklyn Ferry" is a model of the visionary poem. The poet's vision, subjective and objective at once, penetrates the "necessary film" of "appearances" to find revealed patterns of meaning and value that he accepts and loves as "dumb, beautiful ministers," which all "furnish . . . parts toward the soul." The language of the poem may be old-fashioned, but the most generalized aspect of the meaning—that we are not accidental by-products of a lifeless mechanistic universe alien to all human values and meanings—is no more dated than the title of a recent book on the philosophy of science called *Perception and Discovery*. If anything, Whitman's implied concept of vision as at once subjective and objective, with both illusion and discovery always possible, is closer to the current scientific understanding of how we see than is Stevens' sharp dichotomy of imagination and reality.

Whitman's poem starts with the experience of *seeing*. What is seen is *seen as* with the *seeing that* following naturally from the way things are seen. The reader is free to accept the images (the *seen*) and the metaphors (the *seen as*) as fresh and true seeing, as discoveries, even while feeling disinclined to draw the conclusion from them (the *seeing that*) Whitman does.

By contrast, unless the reader shares the belief underlying Stevens' poem, that science ("truth") has revealed that the universe is simply "matter in motion" and thus alien to life and its values, particularly human values, the poem's contrast, section by section, of romantic fancy with naked truth will not strike him as any kind of revelation of the previously unseen but as artful illustrations of a conviction held prior to the experiences described. In Stevens' poem, the eyes seem in the service of the mind, with its beliefs; in Whitman's, the perceived world seems to issue in belief. Stevens' poem is in effect versified epistemology resting on an implied ontology, Whitman's an exercise in fresh vision that has extensions into religious beliefs that the reader need not share in order to feel that the images and metaphors have helped him "learn to see" in depth.

Although it is presumably true, as both vision-laboratory researchers and philosophers of science like von Weizsäcker tell us, that "all perception is theory-laden," yet it is Whitman's poem, not Stevens', that suggests "the unity of nature" and our role as participants. For it is as true for poetry as it is for science that perception requires ideas but also a certain openness to the previously unseen. Discovery, whether in scientific revolutions or in the visionary poems we most value, begins in surmise or guess about the unknown, not in rigid adherence to existing convictions. When it occurs, as it does in Whitman's poem, the previously unseen dawns on us and illuminates some aspect of the world.

★   ★   ★

I hope it has been clear all along that I have not been using "visionary poetry" as a synonym for something like "our finest poetry," but in case it hasn't, I want to be explicit about the matter now. I have tried to define visionary poetry as a literary form clearly enough and narrowly enough so that the concept could be used to exclude as well as include—an aim prompted by my dissatisfaction with what seems to me the widespread current use of *visionary* as a critical term indicating approval without making clear what is being approved. I have both argued and assumed that *visionary* when applied to poetry should be a descriptive term with a reasonably clear content—descriptive, not normative.

So defined, the form has forced the omission from this study of the work of a number of poets who are favorites of mine, three of whom at least are certainly to be considered among our greatest poets, especially Emily Dickinson, Robert Frost, and T. S. Eliot. It may be of course that I have misjudged their work in deciding that it did not fit the visionary mode, in which case others, having a clear standard to apply, should be able to show why I am wrong. But as I see the matter at present, there are sufficient reasons for the exclusions, reasons that have to do with the character of their work, not its value or importance.

I have excluded Emily Dickinson, for example, after a good deal of hesitation and balancing of pros and cons, because I find that typically in the bulk of her work it is thought—thought about what she has seen or felt, believed or failed to believe—that is in control. Very often her poems seem expressions of the arguments she carried on with herself about religious belief and unbelief—Emerson's, or her father's—or about ideas, or about love and death, hope and pain, with the images in the service of the ideas or the feelings. "Arguments": she might have written them up as essays, and she often did write of them, cryptically, in her letters. In them she reasons, setting argument against argument, expressing the arguments in both image and statement. Very often the images are no more than apt illustrations of the thought, as in "I never saw a moor," or missing entirely, as in "Not seeing, still we know," "Lad of Athens, faithful be," and many others.

There are many poems like "Safe in their Alabaster Chambers" in which an unstated argument is carried by the images, and some, not very many but a few of them among her best known and best loved, that appear to satisfy both the formal and the thematic expectations of the visionary poem, discovering positive implications in what can be perceived, poems like "An altered look about the hills" and several of her poems about "circumference," especially "A Route of Evanescence." Sometimes, too, passages in her letters make her sound like a poet who would write more visionary poems than she did, as when she wrote to Higginson that "I was thinking, today—as I noticed, that the 'Supernatural,' was only the 'Natural,' disclosed—" and then illustrated her general statement with two lines of verse: "Not 'Revelation'— 'tis—that waits, / But our unfurnished eyes."

But her restless mind balanced such Emersonian ideas

against their opposites. Perhaps only the innocent eye of the child was permitted to see the "show" going on inside nature's tent, as in "Dew—is the Freshet in the Grass." Or perhaps a winter afternoon's light truly seen would appear only as an affliction, as in "There's a certain Slant of light, / Winter Afternoons." Or the light we see by would fail and darkness would close in, as it does in "I Heard a Fly buzz—when I died," with its terrible last lines, "And then the windows failed—and then / I could not see to see."

Poems like this that move from sharply realized images of sense experience toward interpretation might, I suppose, be described as visionary in form but antivisionary in meaning. Moving her closer to Stevens, they move her further from the visionary company that has been my subject, as do also their thematic counterparts, her late fideistic poems in which religious hope is supported not just by the unseen but by the intrinsically unseeable, as in such poems as "Faith—is the Pierless Bridge," a bridge "too slender for the eye," and "How brittle are the Piers." Dependence on a revelation available only to the faithful has not been typical of American visionary poems. Writing a full-length discussion of her untypical visionary poems might well, I decided, mislead a reader about what to expect of her work as a whole.

★   ★   ★

The case for omitting Robert Frost from my visionary company is even harder to argue for. After his earliest period and before his last, most of his best-known poems begin in observation and move toward interpretation, typically stated in the final lines. He was religious by temperament and on the watch for epiphanies. But two things kept him from being the visionary poet that, with a part of himself, he wanted to be—his natural tendency to skepticism and his intense ambition, the first certainly and the latter probably.

The skepticism that prevented any potential illuminations from being trusted finds expression in "For Once, Then, Something." A lifetime of looking into the darkness for some veritable light had once seemed to be rewarded, but how could one *know*? "What was that whiteness? / Truth? A pebble of quartz? For once, then, something." Since he could never be sure just what he had seen, if he had really seen anything, he found firmer support for his religious faith in the record of past epiphanies granted to others than in his own, as "Sitting by a Bush in Broad Sunlight" suggests. His skeptical mind told him that preoccupation with things eternal at the expense of the empirical was unlikely to result in any significant revelations. The people along the shore who "look at the sea all day" are not likely to be rewarded. But when he himself looked at the land, what he saw was more than likely to be a very dark picture, as time's destructiveness seemed to be almost literally visible in "Spring Pools," or the apparent fortuitousness of natural events was brought to mind by the sight of a white spider on a white heal-all, which, if one thought of Bishop Paley's "argument from design," could have what meaning? "What but design of darkness to appall?— / If design govern in a thing so small."

Or, still looking for a larger pattern of meaning at the edge of the land, near the sea, which buries those it cannot drown, he could take comfort only in the thought that mind could do without any visible support from nature. "Sand Dunes" seems antivisionary in its thrust, with both land and sea suggesting that only in the mind can man find freedom from nature's threat. Lionel Trilling was right when he called Frost a dark poet, though the darkness in Frost's work coexisted with a faith that, though it generally looked in vain for support in experience, persisted and finally found direct expression in the poet's last several volumes, especially in the two masques and the final collection, *In The Clearing*. By this time Frost's fame was secure and he could affort to put all his cards on the table, but it is significant that when he did so it was either dramatically, through Paul in *A Masque of Mercy*, or in the abstractly speculative verse with which he prefaces *In The Clearing*, on the meaning he saw in "God's own descent / Into flesh," that is, the "Incarnation."

Those familiar with the whole body of Frost's work as well as with his life are not likely to find the thought in these lines surprising, except in the directness of its expression. But the evidence that such views were not arrived at only late in life must be looked for chiefly in the biography and the many books based on public readings, talks, and private conversations. We may guess that Frost's shrewd judgment that his career would not have been advanced by such opinions had something to do with his putting them into print only when he felt wholly secure both as a poet and as a sage.

What is too clear to require any guessing is that the revelation alluded to abstractly in these lines had seldom if ever found expression in the many poems that take off from the concretely seen or experienced. Even in the very late poem "A Steeple on the House," in which the early skepticism is missing, the steeple and ordinary life are separated as distinctly as are "soul" and "flesh." A truly visionary poet of the type I have been concerned with would surely not so separate the "house of life" from the "house of worship." Frost maintained his religious faith by what seems like an act of will, not apparently because of but in spite of his personal experience and his reason. His faith bears a closer relationship to the "credo, quia absurdum" position—I believe, because it is absurd—than to the visionary poet's way of seeing and believing.

★ ★ ★

Eliot has so long been out of favor with the younger poets and the critics who take their cue from them that it is rare to find him honored as a "visionary." But if the late work of Yeats and Stevens can be so described, why not that of the Eliot of *The Four Quartets*? Or perhaps an even stronger case could be made for the late Eliot than for the others, since in his later work the belief-system in control requires belief in theological Immanence as well as Transcendence?

I think not, for, though belief-systems dictate the images in the later work of each poet—with Yeats a personally worked-out theosophy based, as he explains in the "Introduction" to *A Vision*, on occult revelations; with Stevens on his readings in philosophy—in *The Four Quartets* the passages that are strongest poetically all speak to us of the ultimate emptiness of private experience. This seems to me to be true even when, or perhaps especially when, the poet is attempting an expression of the doctrine of the Immanence of the divine—that is, when experience of the "seen" reveals the truth of the "unseen." He seems to be contriving such passages only with the aid of Scripture, legend, recondite knowledge, and paradox.

An example of what I mean might be the lyric in "Burnt Norton" beginning "Time and the bell have buried the day." To understand how the sunlight reflected from the glossy blue feathers of the kingfisher may be seen as a reminder of the Christian Revelation, we have to know the association of the fish with Christ in ancient Christian thought, the description of Christ as a "fisher of men" as well as having the power of a king, the significance of the ringing of the bell in the service of the Mass when the ordinary person in the congregation couldn't understand Latin, the fact that another name for clematis is "virgin's bower," and that the yew, an ever-green, was once a symbol of immortality or the life eternal. So heavy a mass of learning and allusion seems to me to leave the actual kingfisher little more than an abstract symbol that need not be attended to very carefully to discover how its meaning is beyond itself in "the still point."

By contrast, the meaning and felt truth of such abstractly prosy passages as the one beginning "Let me disclose the gifts reserved for age" come through much more strongly, requir-ing no erudition to decipher. Although one of the epigraphs for the whole poem has declared the mystic "way up" and "way down" to be "one and the same," the "way down" into darkness seems more truly felt, as in the passage beginning "I said to my soul, be still, and let the dark come upon you / Which shall be the darkness of God." *The Four Quartets* re-mains for me a great and moving poem, but not a "vision-ary" poem belonging in the tradition I have been trying to trace, which is far from exhausting poetry's possibilities.

Poetry can, and does, give expression to all aspects of our experience, not simply the sensuous, so that neither con-ceptual thought nor religious faith is inappropriate to it. Dickinson, Frost, Stevens, and Eliot retain all the eminence we have attributed to them. We just don't describe their work as *visionary*, reserving that word for poetry that remains at-tached to the perceivable world, yet retains positive implica-tions.

Index

Adams, Henry, 190
Aiken, Conrad, 96
"Alien universe," viii–ix, 23, 79, 96–97, 210
American Poets, From the Puritans to the Present, 95
Ammons, A. R., viii, 6, 143–77; *Selected Poems*, 144; *Collected Poems*, 144, 181, 183, 187, 196, 200, 201, 204; and Eliot, 177; and Emerson, 151–52, 156, 169; and Frost, 144; and Roethke, 176, 177; and Whitman, 162, 163, 176–77; and Williams, 176, 177; *A Coast of Trees*, 172–77; "Corsons Inlet," 146, 147, 149–52; *Diversifications*, 171; "Easter Morning," 175–77; "Extremes and Moderations," 170; "Forecast for Today," 172; "For Harold Bloom," 164; "Hibernaculum," 170–71; "Keepsake," 177; "Mirage," 175; "Mountain Liar," 146–47; "Raft," 147, 148–49, 153; "Snowed Last Night a Lot but Warmed up," 172; *The Snow Poems*, 145, 152, 153, 171–72, 183; "So I Said I Am Ezra," 144–45; *Sphere: The Form of a Motion*, 153, 163–69, 171; "Summer Session 1968," 169; *Tape for the Turn of the Year*, 153–63, 169, 171; "They Say It Snowed," 172; "Transcendence," 171; "Turning a Moment to Say So Long," 147; *Uplands*, 169; "Traveling Shows," 173; "Wiring," 174–75
Anderson, Quentin, 46–47
Archetypal images, 4, 9, 114, 134, 135, 149, 191, 203
Arnold, Matthew, 77

Balakian, Peter, 204
Barrett, William, 19–22, 207

Bateson, Gregory, 19–22, 207
"Beats, The," 200–201
Bible, viii, 27, 55, 63, 65, 70, 71, 76, 77, 83, 85, 86, 105, 125, 134, 135–36, 144–45, 151, 172, 173, 194, 195, 217
Bishop Berkeley, 20
"Black Mountain" poets, 200, 201–202
Blake, William, 2, 6, 18, 22, 26, 33, 34, 35, 36, 63, 77, 84, 85, 114, 123, 130, 180, 207; and Whitman, 27–31; "America a Prophecy," 28; "London," 30; "Milton," 85; "Songs of Experience," 30; "Songs of Innocence," 29
Bloom, Harold, 164, 169
Bly, Robert, 202–203
Boehme, Jakob, 202
Bryant, William Cullen, 6; "To a Water Fowl," 11
Buber, Martin, 12
Bucke, R. M., 84
Burroughs, John, 181

Christ, 27, 37, 59–60, 62, 84, 90, 133, 135, 137, 141, 202, 203, 217
Crane, Hart, 6, 67–87, 90, 110, 114, 115, 118–19, 131, 182, 190, 196–97, 206; and Eliot, 73–74, 86; and Whitman, 68, 70, 72–74, 85–86; "Atlantis," 71; "Black Tambourine," 78; *The Bridge*, 68–75, 83; "The Broken Tower," 75–78; "To Brooklyn Bridge" ("Proem"), 68–69, 72; "Cape Hatteras," 68, 72, 73, 74; "Em-

blems of Conduct," 78; "Garden Abstract," 79; "General Aims and Theories," 84–85; "Harbor Dawn," 72; "Lachrymae Christi," 80; "Legend," 78; "For the Marriage of Faustus and Helen," 81; "At Melville's Tomb," 81; "Modern Poetry," 84; "My Grandmother's Love Letters," 78; "North Labrador," 79, 83; "Paraphrase," 80; "Praise for an Urn," 78–79; "Quaker Hill," 73; "Repose of Rivers," 79–80, 83; "Stark Major," 79; "The Tunnel," 69–70; "Van Winkle," 74; "Voyages II," 81–82; "Voyages VI," 82–83; *White Buildings*, 78–84; "Wine Menagerie," 80–81
Critical Guide to Leaves of Grass, A, 51
Cultural symptom, visionary poetry as a, viii, 19, 200, 201, 204–205
Cummings, e.e., 127

Damon, Foster, 84
Dante, 127
"Dead Nature," ix, 23, 79, 96–97
"Deep Image" poets, 200, 202–203
Descartes, 4, 22, 43
Dewey, John, 109
Dickinson, Emily, 6, 212–14, 218; "An altered look about the hills," 213; "Dew—is the Freshet in the Grass," 214; "Faith—is the Pierless Bridge," 214; "How brittle are the Piers," 214; "I

Heard a Fly buzz—when I died," 214; "I never saw a moor," 213; "Not seeing, still we know," 213; "A Root of Evanescence," 213; "Safe in their Alabaster Chambers," 213; "There's a certain slant of light," 214
Donne, John, 18
Dualism, 4, 12, 14–15, 22, 32, 43, 65, 201–202

Eliot, T. S., 7, 73–74, 84, 90–91, 96, 103, 104, 107, 108, 116, 120, 133, 140, 141–42, 177, 180, 181, 183, 192, 200, 212, 217–18; "Burnt Norton," 217; "The Dry Salvages," 177; *The Four Quartets*, 7, 108, 140, 141, 177, 217–18; "A Game of Chess," 104; "Little Gidding," 140, 141; "A Note on War Poetry," 120; "Prufrock," 5; *The Waste Land*, 73–74, 86, 94, 103, 104, 116, 192
Emerson, Ralph Waldo, 2, 3, 6, 18, 40–41, 47, 79, 111, 117, 118, 120, 127, 151–52, 156, 169, 185, 188, 196, 201, 205, 213; "The Bohemian Hymn," 152; "Experience," 40–41; "Illusions," 40; "Nature," 40; "The Poet," 111; "Two Rivers," 188
Empiricism, 26, 31, 180, 188, 215
Epistemology, 5, 20–21, 35, 210, 211
Everson, William, 204
Existentialism, 183
Eye and Brain, 9

Frank, Waldo, 85
Freud, Sigmund, 9, 130
Frisby, John P., 9, 10, 117
Frost, Robert, 6, 96, 118, 144, 200, 205, 212, 214–16, 218; *In The Clearing*, 216; "Design," 215; "For Once, Then, Something," 215; *A Masque of Mercy*, 216; "Sand Dunes," 215; "Spring Pools," 215; " A Steeple on the House," 216

Genre, visionary poetry as a, vii, 18, 206–207, 212
Ginsberg, Allen: "Howl," 200–201, *Howl and Other Poems*, 201
Golden, Arthur, 34
Gregory, R. L., 8–9, 117

Haines, John, 204
Hart Crane: The Life of an American Poet, 85
Heel of Elohim, The, 22–23
Heidegger, Martin, 35
Herbert, George: "Virtue," 13
Higginson, T. W., 213
Hopkins, Gerard Manley, viii
Horton, Philip, 85
Hume, David, 20

Idea of the Holy, The, 82
Illusion of Technique, The, 19
Imagination as noetic, 3–4, 7–9, 10–23, 169
Imagism, 5, 11–12, 14–15, 59, 91, 102, 106, 122, 130
Intelligent Eye, The, 9, 117

James, William, 109, 130
Jeffers, Robinson, 96, 181
Johnson, Samuel, 5, 11, 20; "London," 5, 11
Jung, Carl, 4, 9, 38, 55, 83,191, 203

Kaufman, Lloyd, 9, 117
Kinesthetic perception, 17, 42–43, 54, 117–18, 124, 130, 138
"Kubla Khan," 5

Lawrence, D. H., 117
Letters of Hart Crane, The, 73, 85
Levertov, Denise, 204

Marx, Karl, 180
Materialism, viii, 181
Merton, Thomas, 205
Metaphor, 10–11, 205–206, 211
Metaphysical idealism, 3, 19–21, 40–41, 47, 65
"Metaphysical" poetry, 11, 114, 116, 136
Miller, James, 51, 139
Mills, Ralph, 139
Milton, John, 26–27; *Paradise Lost*, 26
Mind and Nature: A Necessary Unity, 20
Modernism, 18–19, 75, 93, 116, 183, 184, 191, 192, 200
Muir, John, 181
Mysticism, viii, 5, 48, 127, 130, 138–42, 165
Myth, 2, 28–29, 32, 60, 62, 75, 77, 83–85

Naturalism, viii, 21–22, 181, 186
Nature, viii, 46–47, 57–58, 94–95, 114–42 *passim*, 157, 181, 186–93, 196–97
Nietzsche, Friedrich, 114

Oliver, Mary, 204
Olson, Charles, 201–202; "Maximus Poems," 201–202
Ontology, 20, 23, 211
Otto, Max, 82
Ouspensky, P. D., 84

Pack, Robert, 204
Paley, Bishop, 215
"Pathetic fallacy," 17, 23
Perception and Discovery, 211
Perception: The World Transformed, 9, 117
Poe, Edgar Allan, 70, 79, 132, 133, 203
Poetry of meditation, 6, 11, 13
Pope, Alexander, 18
Positivism, viii–ix, 21–23, 158, 181, 207
Pound, Ezra, 12, 14, 117, 200–202; "In a Station at the Metro," 12, 14; *The Cantos*, 201
Process and Reality, 28, 37, 43, 47, 65, 180, 201, 202
"Projective verse," 201–202

Realism, philosophic, 20, 32
Religion, viii, 26, 27, 32, 33, 52–55, 59, 61, 72, 85, 90–91, 100, 110, 122, 127–31, 137, 138–42, 158–62, 164–65, 167–68, 172,

173–74, 175–76, 180–81, 195, 207, 211, 214–15, 216

Religion, Eastern, 144, 171, 173, 204, 205, 206

Rimbaud, Arthur, 80, 84, 85, 183

Robinson, E. A., 96, 181

Roethke, Theodore, viii, 6, 12, 15, 16–18, 19, 23, 113–42, 176, 177, 180, 181, 190, 196, 204; and Crane, 118–19; and Eliot, 116, 133, 140, 141–42; and Emerson, 117, 118, 120; and Frost, 118; and mysticism, 138–42; and Whitman, 114–15, 117–18, 119, 120–21, 127, 131–32, 137, 138, 139, 141; "The Abyss," 114; "Big Wind," 121–22; "Carnations," 122; "Child on Top of a Greenhouse," 122; "Cuttings," 16–18, 23, 119–20, 121–22, 126; "Cuttings (later)," 16–18, 23, 119–20; "The Cycle," 123; "In a Dark Time," 136–37; "The Decision," 138, 139; "The Dying Man," 128–29; *The Far Field*, 126, 127, 138–42; "A Field of Light," 125–26; "The Flight," 124; "Flower Dump," 122; "Four for Sir John Davies," 127; "The Gibber," 124; "I Cry, Love! Love!" 127; "Journey to the Interior," 133–36, 140; "The Longing," 139; "The Long Waters," 140–41; *The Lost Son*, 115, 119–26; "The Lost Son," 123–25, 126, 130; "Meditation at Oyster River," 131–33, 140; "The Minimal," 123; "Moss Gathering," 121; "Night Crow," 123; "Night Journey," 12, 117–19, 138; "North American Sequence," 126, 131, 139–42; "Once More, the Round," 130, 138, 176; *Open House*, 114, 115–19; "The Pit," 124; "Praise to the End," 126–27; "Prayer," 116; "The Restored," 138; "The Return," 124–25; "The Right Thing," 138; "Root Cellar," 120, 121–22; "The Rose," 141–42; "Sequence, Sometimes Metaphysical," 131, 136, 139; "The Shape of the Fire," 126; "The Signals," 116, 117, 119; "Straw for the Fire," 114; "Transplantings," 122; "The Vigil," 127–28; "The Waking," 123, 138; "A Walk in Late Summer," 128

Romantic, 6, 18, 30, 31, 46, 85, 116, 205

Seeing and believing, 6–7, 34–35, 50–51, 114, 116–19, 124–25, 129–30, 138, 146–47, 150–51, 160, 171–72, 173–75, 210–18

Seeing and "seeing as," 10–11, 12, 206, 211

Seeing and thinking, 7–10, 32–33, 211–12, 213–14

Seeing: Illusion, Brain, and Mind, 9, 117

Schorer, Mark, 29

Science and the Modern World, 22, 31

Sight and Mind, 117

Skepticism, ix, 19–21, 36, 40, 41, 64, 158, 169, 180, 190, 214–15, 216

Smart, Christopher, 114, 123

Snyder, Gary, 204, 205, 206

Socrates, 62

Solopsism, 6, 56–57, 207

Stevens, Wallace, 2, 6, 21, 33, 34, 78, 79, 96, 164, 180, 191, 210, 211, 212, 214, 217, 218; "Not Ideas About the Thing, but the Thing Itself," 6; "An Ordinary Evening in New Haven," 6, 210; "Sea Surface Full of Clouds," 210; "The Snow Man," 21, 79, 164

"Surrealist" poetry, 202–203

Symbolism, 84, 85, 86, 114, 131, 183

Thinking and seeing, 7–10, 32–33, 211–12, 213–14

Thoreau, Henry David, 127

Transcendentalism, 136, 152, 171, 186, 188, 196, 197, 205, 206

Trilling, Lionel, 215

Tate, Allen, 86

Taylor, Edward, 18

Technology, viii, 60–61, 62, 73, 204–205

Underhill, Evelyn, 139–42

Unity of Nature, The, 22, 205–206

Vaughan, Henry, 5

Vision research, 3, 8–11; and Whitman, 25, 211, 212

Wagoner, David, viii, 6, 179–97, 210; and Ammons, 183, 187, 196; and Crane, 182, 196–97; and Eliot, 192; and Emerson, 188, 196; and Roethke, 180, 181, 190, 196; and Whitman, 181–83, 185, 196; and Williams, 182–83, 196; "The Bad Fisherman," 192; "Being Shot," 195; "Boy Jesus," 180; *In Broken Country*, 190; "Crossing Half a River," 192; "Do Not Proceed Beyond This Point Without a Guide," 192; "From Here to There," 194–95; "A Guide to Dungeness Spit," 185–86, 191–92; "In the Middle of Nowhere," 192; *Landfall*, 187; "Lost," 192; *Nesting Ground*, 185; *New Poems*, 193; "Night Passage," 192; "Nuthatch," 187–88; "Ode to the Muse on Behalf of a Young Poet," 190–91; "An Offering for Dungeness Bay," 188–90; "Revival," 180; "Riverbed," 192; "A Room With a View," 193; "A Sea Change," 197; "On Seeing an X-Ray of My Head," 187; "Spring Song," 190; "Staying Alive," 192; "Talking to Barr Creek," 192–93; "Tracking," 193–94, 195; "Trying to Pray," 180, 193; "Turning Back and Starting Over," 195–96

Walt Whitman's Blue Book, 34

Weber, Brom, 73

Weizsäcker, C. F. von, 21–22, 205–206

Whitehead, A. N., viii, 22, 23, 28, 31, 32, 37, 43, 47, 65, 79, 109, 180–81, 183, 201, 202, 210

Whitman, Walt, 2, 6, 12, 15–17, 18, 19, 21, 22, 25–65, 127, 131–32, 137, 138, 139, 141, 162, 163, 176–77, 180, 181, 183, 185, 196, 200, 201, 205, 206, 207, 210; and Blake, 27–31; and Crane, 68, 69, 72–74, 78, 83, 84, 85–86; and Roethke, 114–15, 117–18, 119, 120–21; and Williams, 91–92, 94, 96, 111; and Wordsworth, 31–34; "Apparitions," 64; "As I Watch'd the Ploughman Ploughing," 36; "The Base of All Metaphysics," 62–63; "Cavalry Crossing a Ford," 36, 58–59, 94; "Crossing Brooklyn Ferry," 35, 51–53, 63, 210; "Drum-Taps," 56; "Faces," 37–38, 141; "Grand Is the Scene," 29, 108, 176; "When I Heard the Learn'd Astronomer," 36, 57–58; "When Lilacs Last in the Dooryard Bloom'd," 35, 36, 42, 55–56, 94; "The Mystic Trumpeter," 36; "A Noiseless Patient Spider," 12, 15–17, 21, 36, 56–57, 119, 162; "Out of the Cradle Endlessly Rocking," 35, 53–55, 72, 94, 121, 131–32; "Passage to India," 28, 36, 43, 60–62, 71, 73, 108; "To the Sayers of Words," 34; "A Sight in Camp in the Daybreak Gray and Dim," 36, 59–60; "I Sing the Body Electric," 42–44; "I Sit and Look Out," 36, 44–45; "The Sleepers," 44; "Song of Myself," 15, 30, 35, 48–51, 139; "Song of the Open Road," 117, 118; "A Song of the Rolling Earth," 34, 131, 183; "Sparkles from the Wheel," 36; "Starting from Paumanok," 45; "Of the Terrible Doubt of Appearances," 40–41; "There Was a Child Went Forth," 15, 29, 32, 35, 47–48, 54, 57, 63, 121; "To Think of Time," 38–40; "Unseen Buds," 177

William Blake: The Politics of Vision, 29

Williams, William Carlos, 6, 12, 14, 19, 23, 33, 65, 89–111, 155, 176, 177, 181, 182–83, 192, 196, 200, 201, 202; and Crane, 90, 110, 111; and Eliot, 90–91, 96, 103, 104, 105, 107, 108; and the Emerson-Whitman tradition, 111; and nature, 94–97; and objectivism, 91, 102, 106; and religion, 90–91, 100, 115, 119; and Stevens, 96; and Whitman, 91–92, 94–95, 96, 108–10, 111; and Wordsworth, 92; "Asphodel, That Greeny Flower," 105–109, 110; "Between Walls," 92–93; "Chicory and Daisies," 93; "Deep Religious Faith," 100, 110; "The Desert Music," 95, 100–103, 110, 176; "Fine Work with Pitch and Copper," 97–98; "Illegitimate Things," 93–94;

Paterson, 103–105, 201; *Pictures from Brueghel and Other Poems*, 105; "Poem," 12, 14–15; "The Red Wheelbarrow," 93; "Sparrow Among Dry Leaves," 93; "Spring and All," 65, 95–97, 98; "A Unison," 98–100, 101, 103–104

Wittgenstein, Ludwig, 7, 35
Wordsworth, William, 2, 19, 92; and Whitman, 31–34; "Guilt and Sorrow," 34; *The Prelude*, 32, 33

Yeats, W. B., 2, 22, 114, 128, 129, 180, 217; "Sailing to Byzantium," 128–29; *A Vision*, 217